LEEDing
the way

**Domestic
Architecture
for the Future:**
LEED Certified,
Green, Passive
& Natural

E. Ashley Rooney
Contributions by
Ross Cann,
Adam Prince,
and Virge Temme

Schiffer
Publishing Ltd

4880 Lower Valley Road • Atglen, PA 19310

CONTRIBUTORS

Ross Sinclair Cann, AIA, LEED AP, is a historian and educator in Newport, Rhode Island, and the managing director of A4 Architecture. He holds architecture degrees from Yale University, Cambridge University, and Columbia University. He has also taught design and architecture at Parsons the New School for Design, New York University, and the Newport Art Association, and has been a visiting critic at Columbia University, Roger Williams University, and Rhode Island School of Design, among others.

Ross has devoted his career to creating sustainable buildings, including work in historic preservation and adaptive reuse. His firm was recently voted Best Architectural Firm in Newport County by the readers of *Newport Life* magazine. In 2014, the Newport Chamber named it Business of the Year in its size category.

Adam Prince, LEED Green Rater, CSL, is business development principal at Boston-based ZeroEnergy Design. Co-chair of the USGBC Cape & Islands Interest Group, he also champions certifications such as Indoor airPLUS, WaterSense, LEED for Homes, Living Building Challenge, and Passive House. His firm won a design award from the Boston Society of Architects and recently won the Best of Boston's Best Green Architect.

Virge Temme, principal of Virge Temme Architecture, Sturgeon Bay, Wisconsin, has designed hundreds of homes in Illinois and Wisconsin over the past twenty-five years. Specializing in energy-efficient, environmentally responsible buildings, she has been involved in several LEED for Homes projects, ascribes to Passive House modeling, and is a regular newspaper contributor and seminar presenter advocating green building techniques. Her background in historical, Japanese, and energy-efficient architecture, coupled with her long-standing interest in the psychology of space, provides a unique basis for successfully responding to a diverse clientele and a broad stylistic range of projects from historic to modern, all with a primary goal of environmental responsibility.

Front cover: Chester Architecture, @ Keith Brofsky
Back cover: ZeroEnergy Design, @ Michael J. Lee Photography
Front endpaper: Courtesy of Valo Photography
Back endpaper: Courtesy of Kirt Gittings

Copyright © 2015 by E. Ashley Rooney

Library of Congress Control Number: 2015939032

Designed by John P. Cheek
Cover Design by Justin Watkinson
Type set in ITC Avante Garde Gothic/Sabon Lt Std

ISBN: 978-0-7643-4925-6
Printed in China

Published by Schiffer Publishing, Ltd.
4880 Lower Valley Road
Atglen, PA 19310
Phone: (610) 593-1777; Fax: (610) 593-2002
E-mail: Info@schifferbooks.com

For our complete selection of fine books on this and related subjects, please visit our website at www.schifferbooks.com. You may also write for a free catalog.

This book may be purchased from the publisher. Please try your bookstore first.

We are always looking for people to write books on new and related subjects. If you have an idea for a book, please contact us at proposals@schifferbooks.com.

Schiffer Publishing's titles are available at special discounts for bulk purchases for sales promotions or premiums. Special editions, including personalized covers, corporate imprints, and excerpts can be created in large quantities for special needs. For more information, contact the publisher.

CONTENTS

FOREWORD

LEED: A Small History of a Big Step Toward Building Sustainably
Ross Sinclair Cann

The issue of sustainability in transportation and construction is increasingly at the forefront of people's minds. Even a generation ago, nature seemed too great and immovable to ever be affected by a single species populating the Earth. Now, just a geologic blink of the eye later, scientific evidence points strongly to the conclusion that humans are having a marked influence on climate changes and that these changes are coming faster than even the worst predictions of a decade ago. Of all the ways humans use energy, heating and cooling buildings demands the most energy and is a major cause of the greenhouse gases implicated in the rapid and dangerous atmospheric changes. What can we do to veer away from the path that humanity seems so carelessly set upon?

One significant effort is the implementation of LEED standards developed by the US Green Building Council (USGBC), founded in 1993 by Rick Fedrizi, David Gottfield, and Mike Italiano. This small group of volunteers came together to develop best practices that would help designers create buildings that not only use less energy but also were made of longer-lasting, sustainable materials that foster occupants' health and well being.

LEED 1.0, launched in 1998, was a prototype for a program in which points are awarded for meeting standards in selected categories and subject to third-party verification. In 2000, LEED 2.0 established the first certification standards, and the USGBC began certifying buildings that meet the criteria. The program was also intended to encourage other project developers to create more sustainable structures. Since then, the certification program has evolved with building science practices and expanded to other project types. These standards sought to make quantifiable and meaningful improvements in a wide variety of categories, which were the foundation of the

LEED v3/2009 certification:

Sustainable Sites (SS)
Water Efficiency (WE)
Energy and Atmosphere (EA)
Materials and Resources (MR)
Indoor Environmental Quality (IEQ)
Innovation in Design (ID)

Points are awarded in these categories based on a building's improvement over a baseline standard. In many instances, one point is awarded for good performance and two points might be awarded for outstanding performance. In the Energy and Atmosphere (EA) category—a central spine of the program—points accrue as efficiency levels rise.

Early on, the organizers realized that to implement LEED, professionals from many areas of expertise would need to be taught how to apply the standards. Those who seek LEED accreditation must sit for a rigorous test, whether it is the general LEED Green Associate (LEED GA) or a LEED AP exam in a focused area.

LEED standards have evolved with the times. The recently launched LEED v4.0 was a multiyear effort with the more than 150,000 LEED AP and more than 13,000 individual and organization USGBC members contributing ideas about how to make the system better. There are five rating systems that address different project types:

Building Design and Construction (BC+C)
Interior Design and Construction (ID+C)
Building Operations and Maintenance (O+M)
Neighborhood Development (ND)
Homes (H)

Homeowners often ask about the cost premium of building to LEED standards. Most are pleasantly surprised to learn that the additional cost averages two to three percent. But as good design can cut the cost of heating and cooling, reduce water usage, and lessen the need for maintenance and upkeep, the benefits of building green are frequently many times greater than the additional construction cost over the building's lifetime. That means there is not only a strong moral imperative to build more sustainably, but a financial incentive as well. Federal, state, and local tax rebate programs also encourage the building of sustainable structures, which can speed the payback period to three years or less.

Efforts are underway to mandate that operating costs be included in the specifications of houses and buildings for sale. It is a truism that what gets measured will get addressed. This small change on a broad front would add tremendous value to sustainably built structures. Many commercial operations, including hotels and office buildings, make LEED certification a central selling point to attract guests, tenants, and potential owners who want to feel good about their role in reducing carbon emissions.

A building is certified at one of four levels: It must achieve 40 out of a possible 100 points to qualify for the base level, 50 points to achieve LEED-Silver, 60 points for LEED-Gold, and 80 points for LEED-Platinum. At the end of 2012, the USGBC announced that more than 2,000 buildings encompassing more than 4.5 billion square feet in more than thirty countries had been LEED certified. Although this is still a tiny fraction of construction around the world, it has been a tremendous achievement since the first twelve buildings were granted certification in 2000.

It is a telling trend that the sustainable building market in the United States alone is expected to be valued at more than $140 billion in 2015. Yet LEED has not been without controversy. As the standards become widely adopted, some industries, particularly clear-cutting lumber companies, have lobbied against the program. As LEED spreads overseas, however, meeting these standards has become important for manufacturers who export their products. Many have decided it is more productive to join the effort rather than try to protect their short-term interests.

Another approach has been to develop competing standards. The National Association of Home Builders (NAHB) National Green Building Program and the timber industry-supported Green Globes (a program of the Green Building Initiative) are two less rigorous programs for sustainable building. On the other side are those who believe LEED is not demanding enough. The Living Building Challenge, for example, aims for carbon neutral or even carbon negative buildings. This criticism has caused the USGBC to raise its standards along with changes in technology. The growing sense that standards must become both more affordable and more effective is likely to propel changes in the LEED certification process well into the future.

This book illustrates where sustainable building design has been and hints at where it may go in the future. Sustainable buildings need not be expensive, but can be small houses that fit nicely into existing communities. In fact, early colonial structures had many of the same characteristics that the LEED process encourages, such as compact homes on modest sites and in urban neighborhoods.

Fortunately, with the tremendous advance in material technology and construction techniques over the past twenty years, today's homes can be made more energy-efficient and sustainable than at any point in human history. All that is required is a desire to build green, the assistance of knowledgeable designers and contractors, and the confidence that building efficiently will have both environmental and financial benefits. In the wide variety of styles and geographies shown here, I hope that readers will be able to imagine their own projects fitting into this broad spectrum of buildings.

If you have a trained guide on your project, it is not necessary to know the intricate ins and outs of the evolving LEED program. It is enough to know that you want to build a structure that will be healthier not only for its occupants but for the planet, and to be aware that there are systems in the marketplace to help make this aspiration a reality. Every step in the right direction brings us that much closer to a tipping point where building responsibly is not seen as a luxury, but as a necessity. As Margaret Mead so eloquently stated: "Never doubt that a small group of thoughtful, committed citizens can change the world; indeed, it's the only thing that ever has." Fortunately, the number of people looking to build environmentally sustainable structures is growing each day. By reading this book, you are already part of the effort to be well-informed.

Certification: An Expression of Values
Adam Prince

As this compilation of exceptional homes is being released, LEED v4 and Living Building Challenge v3 are being adopted in the marketplace. The mere existence of such certification programs is an expression of collective values, providing perspective on what is important and offering a way to improve today's building practices. In most cases, certifications are optional, so the decision to build in a way that differs from the norm is a deliberate one. The business world often adopts certification standards for operational savings or as a marketing tactic, but the reality is that neither of these motivations can completely account for the groundswell of interest.

The recognition that our actions are the main cause of climate change has encouraged design and construction professionals to consider the role they can play in mitigating environmental damage. A proactive response to this insight helped to shape LEED and other standards. It guided decisions made during the formation of numerous certifications, affecting which potential improvements were most relevant, which should be included, and which should not.

Continually evolving green metrics act as a lens through which we can envision improvements to antiquated construction norms. Whether it is LEED, Passive House, Living Building Challenge, or other certification programs, their role is to empower homeowners and construction professions to "be the change they wish to see."

As certification standards evolve, they are refined and re-interpreted by a larger and larger audience. New iterations embrace feedback from the relevant "community." Where the certification fell short, it is updated and revised. What once was considered progressive may now be considered normal, so the bar is raised.

In many cases, green building standards are used as guidelines, selectively implemented as a best practice. While the checks and balances of third-party certification are missing, selective adoption serves an important role as the marketplace collectively accepts or rejects individual criterion. In time, enough professionals may be convinced of their value to encourage assimilation into building codes. What once was optional now becomes a requirement. What once was progressive is now mainstream. What once was an expression of values and a small proactive initiative can now affect the design and construction of thousands of buildings.

When the opportunity arises to commission, design, or construct a building, consider expressing your values through that decision. You can be certain that choices made now will be reflected over the building's lifespan. Throughout this book are case studies of exceptional homes, some certified, some aspirational, all examples of the power of green building as an expression of human values.

Consider the certifications currently in the marketplace, including LEED for Homes, Passive House, Energy Star, Indoor airPLUS, WaterSense, Living Building Challenge, and others. Are they aligned with your values? Are you going to do only what is legally required, or are you going to "LEED the way," setting a higher standard that helps improve the entire marketplace. Make your choice thoughtfully.

Massive Victorians and McMansions surround my 1830s saltbox. Its windows face roughly south; its rooms are small with low ceilings. Initially, it was only two rooms, but as time went on, the basic design was expanded. To conserve heat, walls and doors were built to separate rooms. Although we certainly have made many changes to the house, we still hang our laundry outside, grow flowers and vegetables, and sit in our garden with friends and family. When my children were younger, they were often playing outside. Despite the many beautifully landscaped terraces and farmer's porches around us, we rarely see anyone outside these days—not even to watch the butterflies dance among the flowers.

The house is no longer just a place to live, but the entire world for many. A national survey by the Kaiser Family Foundation found that with technology allowing nearly twenty-four-hour media access, the amount of time young people spend indoors has risen dramatically. Today, eight- to eighteen-year-olds devote an average of seven hours and thirty-eight minutes to using entertainment media in a typical day (more than fifty-three hours a week). And in the summer they turn up those air conditioners and turn on the apps.

The early American settlers drew upon the prevailing building practices of their native countries, incorporating the building materials available and responding to the local environment. In New England, the settlers turned to wood, and their houses faced south in the hope of acquiring some warmth during the long winter months. Those first houses had only one all-purpose room. As lifestyles progressed, walls and doors were built to separate rooms and conserve heat. Southern houses were built of wood or brick and had elevated first floors and verandas so the residents could enjoy the cooling breezes. In hot, dry regions, they were often built from stone or clay, which offered the best protection against the heat and sun.

The Industrial Revolution ushered in significant enhancements that improved the livability of homes. The former Franklin stove was wrapped in a metal or masonry shell, and ducts conducted the heated air to upper floors. Indoor plumbing, electrical wiring, and asphalt shingles made life easier. But over the years, our homes have become massive structures that keep the environment out and consume large quantities of energy, water, and materials. They often shut out light and air, relying on electric lights rather than daylighting. They depend on air conditioning rather than careful siting and well-planned roof overhangs.

As interest in conservation and concern about the environment grows, many consumers are beginning to consider building a resource- and energy-efficient home. The United States Green Building Council (USGBC) reports that more than 10,000 homes have been certified under LEED for Homes since the program's launch in 2008. Not all homeowners can afford to do all that is necessary for LEED certification, but they can build green homes. The *Wall Street Journal* (5/3/2013) reported that the "Green construction market has grown steadily in recent years. Green housing projects accounted for twenty percent of all newly built homes last year and had an overall value of $25 billion, according to industry-research firm McGraw Hill Construction. As the housing market continues to recover, the researchers predict, this share will grow to between twenty-nine percent and thirty-eight percent of new US homes by 2016."

Resource- and energy-efficient buildings, such as the fifty-three houses found in this book, use sustainable or renewable construction materials to the maximum extent practical. They are designed to be healthy, comfortable, and easy-to live-in residences that make a positive contribution to their communities. The US government is fueling this trend with federal tax credits for things like solar energy and insulation that reduces a home's energy consumption. Depending on where they live, homeowners can also claim rebates from their state or utility. Materials and construction costs for these homes can increase their price, but the extra cost is usually offset in the long term by lower utility bills. A 2012 study by two professors at the University of California, Berkeley, and the University of California, Los Angeles, found that homes in California with a green label sell for about nine percent more than a comparable conventional house.

Today, most houses that meet the USGBC's definition of a green home (use less energy and fewer natural resources and toxic chemicals) look like their neighbors. They, too, are country cottages, waterfront homes, and desert contemporaries, but they generally sell quickly and for more money than other houses on the block.

Respectful of nature and its resources, the twenty-nine architects and builders included here describe how to create a comfortable home. Many of the homes were pioneers of sustainable building in their region. Some are owned by the architect. In all cases, the objective is to build homes that reduce energy consumption and harmonize with their natural environment.

Let it not be for present delight nor for present use alone. Let it be such work as our descendants will thank us for. —John Ruskin

LEED for Homes–Platinum

LEED is a point-based system where building projects earn points for meeting specific criteria (see Ross Cann's Foreword). Within each category, projects must satisfy particular prerequisites to be considered for certification, and credits are given for a range of optional improvements. Certification level depends on the number of points the project earns. A building can receive as few as 40 or as many as 110 points, as follows:

Platinum   80 points and above
Gold   60–70 points
Silver   50–59 points
Certified   40–49 points

If you wish to build a LEED-certified house, your builder must document that the standards were followed.

CHAPTER 1

Opposite: *Courtesy of Jack Coyier*

Net Zero Energy Home and Sustainable Farm

Escondido, California
Hubbell & Hubbell Architects

▼ The home sits between the swimming pool and entertaining patio on the west and the vegetable garden on the east. A solar-powered geothermal heat pump heats and cools the home and also heats the pool. The geothermal system uses the ground as a heat source or heat sink. Any waste heat from the heat pump is sent to the hot water heater, reducing the need to burn natural gas. *Photography ©2014 Philipp Scholz Rittermann*

▼ The clients asked for a net zero energy home to accompany their sustainable farm in the hopes of achieving a carbon-neutral footprint. Hubbell & Hubbell Architects oriented the 2,620-square-foot building to maximize natural daylighting, ventilation, and exposure of the rooftop solar panels, which power the entire home and two plug-in hybrid cars. The airy four-bedroom, three-and-a-half-bath home celebrates the scenic view of Lake Hodges and takes advantage of the Mediterranean climate by blurring the line between the indoors and outdoors. Decks and roofs extend over western-facing windows to shade them from the hot afternoon sun.

▲ Interior finishes were carefully selected for their low-impact attributes. Materials include bamboo and cork flooring, concrete and recycled-glass countertops, and non-VOC paints. Smart-home technology helps efficiently control everything from lighting to landscape irrigation.

▲ A glass hallway bridges the public living space and the more private office and bedroom wing. Operable windows follow the stairs on the east side. In the summertime, the windows draw cool air in low. The tower acts as a solar chimney by drawing the hot air up and out of the home. *Courtesy Alex Miller*

▲ The house's building envelope is an important part of its energy performance. Walls are made of 1-foot-thick insulated concrete form (ICF) blocks made of recycled concrete and Syrofoam® that also resist fire, termites, and mold. The architects designed the house around the blocks' modular dimensions to minimize construction waste and labor costs. Shown here is the owners' electric car, being charged with electricity produced from the sun. The San Diego AIA awarded this project Energy Efficient Home of the Year in its California Green Homes Program.

▲ Bi-fold doors open the living and dining rooms out onto the covered pool patio. A deciduous passion fruit vine helps control late afternoon sun in the summer months and allows for passive heating in the winter. *Photography ©2014 Philipp Scholz Rittermann*

Skyline Residence
Portland, Oregon
Nathan Good Architects PC

▼ Nathan Good Architects designed the 4,200-square-foot residence to optimize natural light to the interior. Systems are in place for future rainwater harvesting, and 100 percent of the storm water is managed on-site. The drought-tolerant landscape is low maintenance. *Courtesy of Bitterman Photography*

▲ Bands of clerestory windows wrap the great room, providing soft natural light from above. An open floor plan facilitates casual living and family cohesiveness. The ceiling's wood beams came from a home that previously existed on the site. *Courtesy of Bitterman Photography*

▲▲ A generous covered patio room graces the south side of the home. The curved plaster wall that extends from the entry of the home, through the entry hall, and out the far side organizes the various rooms on the interior like the string in a strand of pearls. *Courtesy of Bitterman Photography*

▲ High windows and high ceilings let natural light flow into the bathroom. Walnut cabinets lend a sense of warmth. Most of the home's building materials were sourced within a 500-mile radius of the property. *Courtesy of Bitterman Photography*

▲ The gallery on the second floor floods the lower floor levels with natural light and connects the children's rooms with the living spaces below. Healthy indoor air quality is maintained with allergen filters and the use of a heat recovery ventilator. *Courtesy of Bitterman Photography*

▲ Solar panels are mounted across the upper roof. Windows were carefully sized to maximize natural light and views to the surrounding property. *Courtesy of Bitterman Photography*

Beach Residence
Newport Beach, California
LivingHomes

▼ The LivingHome KT1.5, designed by KieranTimberlake, was the first home to be certified LEED-Platinum in Newport Beach, California. Floor-to-ceiling windows bring natural light deep into the space. *Courtesy of Scott Mayoral*

▲ The 2,140-square-foot home includes natural, non-toxic, and sustainably derived materials, including a SunTech America photovoltaic system, Andersen composite wood recycled window frames, and Owens Corning forty percent recycled glass content blown-in insulation. The home has two bedrooms and two and one-half baths with Kohler dual-flush toilets and low-flow fixtures. *Courtesy of Scott Mayoral*

Urban Loft
Portland, Maine
Richard Renner | Architects

◄ This derelict commercial building found new life as an ultra-efficient live/work space in a mixed-use neighborhood. The lower level houses the offices; above is a loft containing two bedrooms, a study, and a TV/guest room—an ambitious program for 1,400 square feet. The owners were determined to build responsibly without compromising design quality. The loft entrance was relocated to the side street to increase privacy. Planted canopies delight passersby, and the storefront displays office projects and the work of local artists. The project received a Citation for Design in the Boston Society of Architects Housing Design Awards. *Courtesy of James R. Salomon*

◤ The study is located in the space created by punching up through the roof. The owners designed and detailed the railings and stair; the raw steel (protected by wax to retain its original patina) celebrates the fabrication process. High windows here bring south light into areas that are not near windows and provide passive ventilation. A custom-designed folding steel ladder leads to a roof deck and the vegetated roof while preserving working space in the study below. An extended landing creates additional counter space. The custom cabinet below the stair landing can be moved into the room for entertaining. Photos by the owner and artist friends are displayed throughout. *Courtesy of Peter Vanderwalker*

► The loft's entire length is on view from the master bedroom. Recycled sliding glass doors separate the second bedroom (currently used as an exercise room) from the hall. Light tubes illuminate the bathroom, located on the interior wall. A small gas boiler supplies heat to the radiant flooring and on-demand hot water heater. Fresh air circulates via a heat recovery ventilator. *Courtesy of Peter Vanderwalker*

◀ Inside, the tightly organized plan accommodates all required functions without compromising openness and long interior views. The interiors capitalize on the building's odd shape. The new entrance replaces what was once a loading dock. A tall pantry helps define the kitchen. Environmentally responsible materials include recycled doors, low- or no-VOC paints, tiles with recycled content, locally sourced wood floors, recycled steel, bamboo plywood cabinets, and Paperstone® counters. *Courtesy of Peter Vanderwalker*

▶ The loft achieved a HERS rating of 43 and came close to meeting the Thousand Home Challenge energy standards. Thanks to the 1-kilowatt solar panel and super-tight building envelope (walls R-35, roof R-55), including triple-glazed fiberglass windows, the loft consumed only 20.3 kBtu-per-square-foot per year during its first year. Heat and hot water costs were just $360. *Courtesy of Peter Vanderwalker*

Tiburon Bay House
Tiburon Bay, California
Butler Armsden Architects

▶ Thanks to the close collaboration between builder and architect, this home earned 113.5 LEED points, exceeding the 91 points required for Platinum level. An exterior bridge serves as an outdoor living space and connects the home's main living area to the upper garden terrace. Windows and exterior doors were made close by—the windows in San Francisco and the doors in Los Angeles—and positioned for horizontal and vertical air movement. Natural oil-and-water-based stain protects the FSC-certified western red cedar siding. *Courtesy of Matthew Millman Photography*

▼ The team analyzed sun studies to determine the optimal window size and location, roof slope and overhangs, and building orientation. A 5-kilowatt photovoltaic system supplements the home's passive heating and cooling, bringing energy consumption to net zero. *Photo courtesy of Matthew Millman Photography*

▲ To minimize circulation space and plumbing and mechanical runs, the architects came up with a pinwheel floor plan that spirals out from a staircase and hidden mechanical room, taking advantage of views of the drought-tolerant garden and San Francisco Bay. The stairs' custom-fabricated metalwork is made of approximately ninety percent recycled material. Lumber is FSC-certified and treated with an ultra-low-VOC stain. *Courtesy of Matthew Millman Photography*

▛ Most of the materials came from vendors located within a 500-mile radius. Heath Ceramics tile used in the master bath came from the next town over, Sausalito. Plumbing fixtures and fittings are highly efficient. Dual-flush toilets average 1.1 gallons of water per flush, showers use 1.75 gallons of water per minute, and faucets use 1.5 gallon per minute. A 3,400-gallon rainwater harvesting tank supplies water for the toilets and washing machines. Graywater is collected from the sinks, showers, and washing machine to irrigate the garden. A solar hot water system provides 100 percent of domestic hot water needs. *Courtesy of Matthew Millman Photography*

◀ Countertops contain eighty percent recycled glass, and appliances are Energy Star rated. The Henrybuilt kitchen cabinet system was chosen for its high percentage of FSC-certified wood, use of renewable resources, high construction quality, durability, and the Seattle manufacturer's relative proximity to the site. *Courtesy of Matthew Millman Photography*

▲ Several LEED points came from the use of permeable hardscaping, the graywater irrigation system, and the use of drought-resistant plants, like the lush native lawn pictured here. In addition, the site plan preserved the lot's natural topography to minimize excavation. Demolition of an existing house involved reusing or recycling ninety-five percent of the materials. A gabion retaining wall and concrete pavers on the lower-level patio were constructed with materials from the demolition site, which reduced transportation requirements and the need to buy new materials. *Courtesy of Matthew Millman Photography*

Vermont Platinum
Charlotte, Vermont
Pill-Maharam Architects

▲ The goal of this 2,800-square-foot project was to create a house with as little environmental impact as possible while maintaining a high level of design and detail. The house takes its cues from its rural context of barns and farmhouses. *Photos courtesy of Westphalen Photography*

▲▶ An open plan brings southern daylight into every living space. The ground-source heat pump, high-performance lighting and appliances, and a 10-kilowatt net-metered wind turbine enable the house to generate as much energy as it uses and achieve zero carbon emissions. *Courtesy of Westphalen Photography*

▶ Simple massing, smart solar orientation, and a well-insulated building envelope helped this house earn LEED's highest rating—the first in Vermont. The home is also 5+ Energy Star rated and Vermont Green certified. *Courtesy of Westphalen Photography*

◀ The terra-cotta-colored fiber-cement boards are one of the home's more modern expressions. The panels are installed as a rain screen system, which has advantages in waterproofing and blocking unwanted heat gain compared to traditional wall systems. These durable panels resist termites and mold, and their integral color means that scratches will never have to be painted. Fiberglass windows also lower the home's environmental impact by creating a virtually maintenance-free exterior. *Courtesy of Jack Coyier*

▼ Indoor-outdoor living and the efficient use of space are important elements in small homes located in the mild Southern California climate, yet the existing home had small rooms that did not connect well to the outside. The use of sight lines, color, and natural light created a home where the exterior space is an extension of the interior and vice versa. The gracious central hallway may at first seem odd for a home that is on such a tight footprint, yet the hallway ties the house together with light and views and provides functional space for the laundry closet. *Courtesy of Jack Coyier*

◀ Architect Kyle Moss renovated this home for his family after completing several projects in the LEED for Homes pilot program. He added a partial second floor to a modest Spanish-style house, increasing it from 1,400 to 2,100 square feet. A canted wall and a cantilevered bed alcove join smooth-finish stucco and terra-cotta tiles in a harmonious blend of traditional Spanish and contemporary design. *Courtesy of Jack Coyier*

◀ Shoe cubbies by the front door are one of the many small, thoughtful details; they did away with the large, messy piles of shoes by the door. Now all the family members have their own discreet cubby. The cubbies earned a LEED point for indoor contaminant control, which is part of the Indoor Environmental Quality category. *Courtesy of Jack Coyier*

▲ The stairs' translucent railing panels, embedded with gingko leaves and reeds, bring daylight and nature to the center of the house. The architect used strand bamboo for the treads, and shower door hardware to attach the railing panels to the ceiling. Convection currents are funneled up the stair and exhausted through clerestory windows to vent the home passively and eliminate the need for air-conditioning in the mild coastal climate. *Courtesy of Jack Coyier*

▼ A spacious kitchen and dining area opening to a deck replaced the small, outdated galley kitchen. Green features include the counter made of fifty-five percent recycled material, a recycled glass backsplash, and Energy Star rated appliances, as well as the strand bamboo flooring, no-VOC paint, and LED lighting. With easy access to the family's vegetable garden, ample workspace for multiple chefs, and a relaxed indoor/outdoor plan that welcomes guests, the kitchen is the heart of the new home. *Courtesy of Jack Coyier*

New Mexico Platinum
Corrales, New Mexico
Krupnick Studio

▲ When builder Brian C. Freeman constructed a contemporary home among the sand hills in Corrales, New Mexico, his goal was to create something vernacular, low-impact, and humble. While the 3,017-square-foot residence is highly energy- and resource-efficient, its green features do not overwhelm the sense of home. The rugged yang of concrete block walls, raw steel beams, honed concrete floors, a photovoltaic system, solar hot water, and corrugated metal coexist with the sensual and human: natural plaster walls, classic modern furniture, handmade art, and environmentally and socially conscious materials. The house also harvests rainwater and reuses graywater. To "live in balance" became the push and pull of the design/build process. *Courtesy of Kirt Gittings*

▼ Architect Michael Krupnick designed a house that embraces the natural environment and distant mountain views. The grand overhang has a dual function: it meets the morning sun and shields the house from excessive heat gain. *Courtesy of Kirt Gittings*

◀ A brise soleil protects the entry from the western sun; there is just one small window on the west. The detached barn/solar power plant is tucked behind the main house. Glass overhead doors allow the barn to be passively heated in the winter. *Courtesy of Kirt Gittings*

▲ *Courtesy of Kirt Gittings*

▲ *Courtesy of Kirt Gittings*

▲ Centrally located, the hearth heats the home and is surrounded by FSC-certified basswood plywood ceilings and walnut cabinets. The owner's father purchased the 100-year-old walnut for the barn door (in the background) at auction twenty-five years ago. *Courtesy of Kirt Gittings*

▲ The table was made from reclaimed monkey wood and salvaged walnut planks. *Courtesy of Kirt Gittings*

▲ All rooms are connected by a visual axis. The kitchen, with its recycled quartz countertops, is the center of daily life. *Courtesy of Kirt Gittings*

▼ Just off the master bath is an outdoor shower heated by a roof-mounted solar hot water tank. The electricity is harvested with 4.3-kilowatt photovoltaic collectors on the barn roof. *Courtesy of Kirt Gittings*

▼ The window seat in the trombe wall is the best place to sit on a quiet winter day. *Courtesy of Kirt Gittings*

Kansas Platinum
Kansas City, Kansas
Studio 804

▲ 3716 Springfield was Studio 804's second project that involved using parts from a warehouse deconstruction at the Sunflower Ammunition Plant in De Soto, Kansas. Abandoned since 1992, the 9,065-acre site is undergoing a decontamination process of approximately 1,000 retired ammunition buildings from volatile toxins and explosives. Reclaimed seventy-year-old Douglas fir from one of the buildings was used to form the roof's scissor truss. The deconstructed warehouse also yielded wood material for wall surfaces, shelving, and other unique features.

▲ The building exterior features a vertical wood rain screen made of FSC-certified South American hardwood, which typically has a fifty-plus-year lifecycle. Exterior walls are stuffed with wet-pack blown cellulose insulation, giving the assembly an R-20 insulation value. The ceiling contains a minimum of twelve inches of blown cellulose yielding an R-38 insulation value.

▲ The galley-style kitchen opens toward an exterior south-facing expanse of glass. The louvered shading system blocks excessive sunlight during the summer and allows heat gain during the winter. Studio 804 elected to use epoxy-coated concrete for the ground floor because of concrete's ability to absorb winter sunlight, thereby reducing the building's energy consumption. Operable windows are low to the ground, allowing air to naturally ventilate upward to skylights and second-story windows.

▼ In the future, the house will include a graywater system and solar panels that send energy back to the electrical grid through net metering. A geothermal heat pump uses constant temperatures below grade to reduce the building's heating load. The first-story radiant floor slowly releases heat set to a thermostat, focusing the heat at the first six feet above the floor. This building was a prototype for the region as the first LEED-Platinum home in Kansas.

▼▼ A broad southern exposure makes the best use of passive solar principles, so the long and narrow building was placed along an east-west axis toward the site's northernmost edge. A double-height western atrium expanded the living spaces into the wooded reserve to the west. The high ceiling draws the air upward to exit through operable skylights on the northern roof face.

Belles Townhomes
San Francisco
LivingHomes

▲ The project features flexible interior layouts, recycled and reused materials, and lighting and appliances that minimize energy use. *Courtesy of Rick Chapman*

◄ Designed by KieranTimberlake for the modular company LivingHomes, Belles Townhomes was the first multi-family project in San Francisco to be certified LEED-Platinum. Each of the seven, three-story attached units includes a garage, patio, and rooftop deck overlooking a shared green and wooded area. *Courtesy of Rick Chapman*

Cannon Beach Residence

Cannon Beach, Oregon
Nathan Good Architects PC

▶ The Cannon Beach residence uses a solar-electric and solar-thermal system and a ground-source heat pump. Nathan Good Architects designed the 2,268-square-foot home to produce as much energy on site as it consumes annually. A band of clerestory windows scoops natural light to the middle of the great room. *Courtesy of Greg Kozawa Photography*

◀ The great room's curved roof also shades a covered porch along the south side of the home. Wind-fallen incense cedar logs were repurposed as columns for the porch roof. *Courtesy of Greg Kozawa Photography*

▲ Vegetation on the upper roof reduces the rainwater runoff on the site and helps the house blend with the hillside when viewed from neighboring properties above. A curved wall at the main entry welcomes residents and visitors. *Courtesy of Greg Kozawa Photography*

▲ An incense cedar log anchors stairs to the loft and roof deck. A tree on the property supplied the stair's wood supports. A large boulder brought to the site for the fireplace wall was left in place and now serves as a seat and a climbing attraction for kids. *Courtesy of Greg Kozawa Photography*

▲ More than ninety percent of the wood used on the home's construction and interiors came from FSC-certified sources. The old stove was salvaged from the client's childhood home and refurbished to meet current energy and safety criteria. *Courtesy of Greg Kozawa Photography*

▲ The bathroom floor was inspired by the edge of the seashore where waves lap over pebbles and sand, and the refinished clawfoot tub invites luxurious baths. *Courtesy of Greg Kozawa Photography*

Illinois Platinum
Glencoe, Illinois
Kipnis Architecture + Planning

▶ A challenging site led to the home's design of two south-facing volumes that connect on the second floor. This computer image shows the differing angles used on the roof to optimize the solar panels and still allow passive solar into the house. The wider roof area in the center helps collect water for the green roof. A dormer in the center of the courtyard provides opportunities for natural ventilation. The different types of solar panels are set at their optimal angle for maximum power production.

▼ The rear view of the 5,200-square-foot house shows the standing seam metal roof set at an optimal angle for the solar thermal panels. Barely visible to the left is the other roof form, set at a lower angle for the PV panels. Overhangs are designed for winter sun penetration and summer shading. *www.scottbellphotography.com*

44

▲ A covered front porch helps reduce the house's scale in keeping with the neighboring homes. Its proportions are traditional, while the color, materials, and detailing are modern. For example, the windows have divided lights that acknowledge the double-hung windows typical of a traditional farmhouse. They are actually casement windows, chosen for their maximum tightness and efficiency. *www.scottbellphotography.com*

▶ Unlike many green roofs, this second-floor roof is an integral part of the home, visible and accessible from both the master bedroom and main hallway. The large quad sliding patio doors open the master bedroom to the planted roof. From there, the owners can easily remove snow from the photovoltaic panels, visible at the roof edge. *www.scottbellphotography.com*

▼ Furnishings and finishes live lightly. The wood flooring is an engineered wide-plank product made from reclaimed barn wood. The super-efficient fireplace is a sealed combustion/direct vent system with a fully gasketed door. FLOR carpet (not shown) can be recycled at the end of its life. The automated HVAC system is controlled via the TV and phone or tablet.

The home achieved a HERS rating of 32, which means it uses only use 32 percent of the energy of a standard new home.

Passive/Active Solar Home

Leawood, Kansas
DRAW Architecture + Urban Design

▶ This 2,520-square-foot passive/active solar home was the first privately funded, single-family residence in Kansas to earn a LEED Platinum certification. Because of a compromised foundation, the site's existing house was deconstructed, and eighty-two percent of its materials were recycled or repurposed. Data on the solar orientation, prevailing winds, and mature tree canopy helped to inform the design. R-values up to 60 significantly reduce energy costs and contribute to the house's nearly net zero performance. *Courtesy of Sharon Gottula Photography*

▲ The owners asked for a house that would allow them to reconnect with the natural environment. The south-facing solarium provides this connection while expanding the interior living space during temperate weather. Thick concrete flooring collects, stores, and distributes the sun's heat in the winter and reflects solar heat in the summer. *Courtesy of Sharon Gottula Photography*

▲ A ground-source heat pump provides heating, air conditioning and hot water while using roughly fifty percent less energy than a standard furnace system. In addition to R-40 SIPs construction, the house has energy-efficient windows with an R-value of at least 6. A 4-kilowatt solar panel system was integrated into the concrete tile roof, and a rainwater catchment system provides irrigation for low-maintenance native plantings. *Courtesy of Sharon Gottula Photography*

▲ The kitchen transitions into the living space. *Courtesy of Sharon Gottula Photography*

▲ The new home is clean, modern, and filled with natural light. *Courtesy of Sharon Gottula Photography*

First Platinum in Maine
Freeport, Maine
Richard Renner | Architects

▶ Designed as a spec house to showcase sustainable building principles, this 3,000-square-foot, four-bedroom home is located on a two-acre wooded lot in an existing subdivision. Richard Renner Architects oriented it true south to minimize site disruption and maximize solar gain. Aesthetically, it walks a line between appealing to a wide range of potential buyers and expressing its eco-friendly values.

▲ Generous overhangs keep water away from walls and shade windows from the summer sun. A rain screen ensures that when siding does get wet, it dries completely as a result of air circulating behind it. Solar panels and solar hot water collectors are installed on the roof. Much of the energy efficiency comes from the high-performance building envelope. Almost all framing lumber and trim is FSC-certified, and the builder used a twenty-four-inch framing layout that aligns studs, floor joists, and trusses to eliminate labor redundancy and reduce waste.

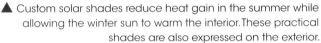

▲ Custom solar shades reduce heat gain in the summer while allowing the winter sun to warm the interior. These practical shades are also expressed on the exterior.

▶ The open plan makes the interior feel larger. Eco-friendly choices include FSC-certified flooring, framing, trim, and millwork; materials that have recycled content or are locally produced or extracted; and low- or no-VOC finishes. Doors feature a rapidly renewable wheat-based core with a wood veneer and use low-VOC adhesives and finishes. The house also has an Energy Star Advanced Lighting Package.

▲ Triple-glazed windows reduce heat loss. Heat from the boiler is distributed through radiant floors, and a heat recovery ventilator provides fresh air. The solar hot water system is designed to direct excess heat to the heating system, covering most of the heating load in the "shoulder" months. Passive solar gain in the winter also plays a role in lowering heating demand. The house received a HERS rating of 42.

Platinum Shoebox
Santa Fe, New Mexico
Praxis Design/Build

▼ In collaboration with his clients, architect Gabriel Browne designed this 1,760-square-foot custom home to prove that it is possible to build an earth-friendly home on a tight budget. Construction costs totaled $188 per square foot upon completion in late 2010, and the dramatic thrust of the second floor living space and gallery proves that limited finances do not preclude dramatic design. *Photo by Laurie Allegretti*

▲ The clients affirmed their home's regional flavor by preserving the old adobe wall at the entrance to their co-housing community, serving as a striking counterpoint to the twenty-first-century home immediately behind. The wall is a tip of the hat to mud bricks, one of the most earth-friendly building materials still in use today. Bright red stucco announces the entrance, sheltered from the elements by the second-floor overhang housing the living space, gallery, kitchen, and guest quarters. *Photo by Laurie Allegretti*

▲ Ordinary materials, such as corrugated steel culverts and used bowling balls, create a memorable xeriscape garden in the courtyard between the master bedroom and studio. The upended culverts serve as reservoirs for storm water and snow runoff from the roof canales. The water is fed into an irrigation system that waters the plants and trees in this arid climate. *Photo by Laurie Allegretti*

◀ The second floor displays exotic folk art objects that the clients collected while working for the US State Department. *Photo by Laurie Allegretti*

▲ The creative use of a small, awkward infill lot, which had been vacant for years, earned the project 2 of its 88 LEED points, and the lot constraints dictated its distinctive design. Browne turned traditional living spaces upside down. The master bedroom and work studios are on the ground floor; living, dining, kitchen, and guest areas are on the second level. Strategically placed and sized windows provide light without compromising privacy. Other points were awarded for extra insulation, an efficient heating system, high-efficiency plumbing fixtures, and efficient irrigation, among other features. The project won the AIA Santa Fe Distinguished Building and Urban Design Award in 2011, as well as Energy Star and AirPlus designations. *Photo by Laurie Allegretti*

◀◀ Project superintendent John McDonough handcrafted this shower stall in the upstairs guest bathroom from galvanized sheet metal. *Photo by Laurie Allegretti*

◀ The compact kitchen reflects the clients' many years abroad that made them appreciate the efficiencies of smaller kitchens. The design collaboration between Browne and his clients went halfway around the world via SketchUp, a 3D program that allowed the owners to "walk through" design models as they worked on other continents. *Photo by Laurie Allegretti*

Historic Neighborhood
Athens, Georgia
Bork Design

▼ This modern, 2,632-square-foot home manages to blend into its historic mill house neighborhood. The front facade brings the scale down to that of smaller neighboring cottages, and the glassy south-facing facade uses porch roofs and deep gable overhangs to control sunlight coming into the home. *Courtesy of Bettie Maves*

▲ The home grows larger in the rear. Here, a covered patio and the second-floor screened porch protect the large patio doors, encouraging natural ventilation and outdoor unconditioned living. The aluminum-clad wood windows and doors are durable and Energy Star certified. North- and east-facing clerestory windows bring natural light into the master bedroom and bathroom above. The roof's butterfly shape provides more south-facing surface area for mounting the solar hot water panel. *Courtesy of Bettie Maves*

◀▲ Windows in the vaulted front room funnel natural light deep into the open living area. The wood-paneled bookcase was built from pine siding reclaimed from an old storage shed on-site. As many materials as possible were recycled in the shed's demolition. The teak on the island bar counter and custom media cabinet came from the owner's previous home in Costa Rica. Beyond the bookcase, reclaimed Georgia heart pine floors step down to exposed, sealed-concrete floors. The slab was poured with twenty percent recycled flyash, a by-product of coal burning. *Courtesy of Bettie Maves*

▶ Skylights and large windows bring natural light into the stairway and entry. The operable skylight above the loft office at the top of the stair pulls fresh air up through the house. Zero-VOC, mineral-based paints from ROMA Eco-Sustainable Building Technologies were used throughout the home, and all polyurethanes and stains are low-VOC. *Courtesy of Bettie Maves*

▼ The landscape minimizes turf and includes only native, drought-tolerant plants. Aluminum rain chains hanging from the porch roof terminate at collection boxes within the built-in block planters. Perforated pipe runs through the planters, providing natural irrigation with an overflow into a front rain garden filled with iris and asters (the darker mulch area). Other downspouts also drain into the rain garden. The home and landscape are designed to keep all storm water on-site. *Courtesy of Bettie Maves*

▲ An 1,100-gallon cistern collects rainwater from over thirty percent of the roof area. The downspout along the side carport is piped to an underground cistern and then pumped to a drip system irrigating the front yard vegetable garden. The rear roofline's butterfly shape helps direct runoff to the downspouts; its Galvalume® metal roofing is Energy Star labeled and highly reflective to prevent it from heating up in the sun. The house received an Athens Clarke Heritage Foundation Award for Outstanding New Construction in a Historic Neighborhood and a USGBC Georgia Athens Branch 2013 Green Building Award. *Courtesy of Bettie Maves*

Prairie Style
Willmar, Minnesota
Green Lyfe

▼ The Green Lyfe Home, a collaborative effort of Phil Anderson, Jeff Nagel, and Julie Alsum, was designed to show that building green does not have to cost much more than conventional construction. This prairie style home fits beautifully into its residential neighborhood. True to its roots, it has a low-slope roof with wide overhangs that shade windows to reduce solar heat gain in summer while allowing winter sunlight to penetrate. The entry surface is flat, allowing for easy accessibility. Exterior lighting is on a photocell, and a CO detector activitates garage ventilation. Drought-resistant plantings minimize water usage. *Courtesy of Mark Peterson*

▲ SIPs exterior walls offer maximum R-values while reducing air infiltration and minimizing the amount of wood used in construction. Solar panels on the roof provide hot water for domestic use and for the in-floor heat system on the lower level. Fiber-cement siding, pre-finished off-site, clads the exterior. Durable, thermally insulated windows allow plenty of daylight into the interior. The insulated concrete foundation (ICF), covered with a stucco finish, provides high R-value and sound-deadening qualities to ensure a quiet, comfortable interior. Half of the rainwater falling on the roof is collected in a lower-level holding tank and used for irrigation or other non-potable purposes. Any extra water from the site is piped to a rain garden. *Courtesy of Mark Peterson*

◀ Quartz and solid-surface countertops contain recycled material, and the cork flooring is renewable and comfortable underfoot. Faucets are WaterSense-certified, and a graywater reuse system connects to the main floor bath. A customizable lighting and sound system allows for the connection of a portable music player. *Courtesy of Mark Peterson*

▶ Eleven-foot-high ceilings enhance the living room's abundant natural light. LED recessed light fixtures in the living area and compact fluorescent lighting in all other areas reduce energy costs. The home also has three tubular skylights, one in the lower-level bath, so that natural light fills every room. *Courtesy of Mark Peterson*

◀ Stairs double back to the lower level, providing access to an exterior on-grade paver patio from the stair landing. The pavers are made with seventy-five percent recycled materials, primarily from tires and plastic milk containers. A door off the dining area leads out to a cedar deck overlooking the backyard. *Courtesy of Mark Peterson*

First Platinum Home in the Nation
Santa Monica, California
LivingHomes

▲ This three-bedroom RK1 LivingHome, designed in 2006 by Ray Kappe, was the first home in the nation to be certified LEED-Platinum. The 2,500-square-foot LivingHome model home achieves zero energy, zero water, zero waste, zero carbon, and zero emissions, proving that less is indeed more. © *Tom Bonner*

▲ The open downstairs has multiple floor-to-ceiling sliders that allow for natural light and ventilation. © *Tom Bonner*

▲ The first home in Los Angeles County to have a permitted graywater system, it recycles water from sinks and showers to irrigate the landscape's drought-tolerant plants. © *Tom Bonner*

▲ An evacuated-tube solar hot water collector supplies hot water for household use and an in-floor radiant heating system. The home is mainly powered by a 2.4-kilowatt solar photovoltaic canopy, which doubles as a shading structure for the roof garden. © *Tom Bonner*

Vineyard Residence
Yamhill County, Oregon
Nathan Good Architects PC

▼ Nathan Good Architects sited this 4,100-square-foot residence to overlook the vineyards and optimize solar exposure to the interior and photovoltaic array. The roof tiers reflect the rows of grapevines along the hillside. *Courtesy of Daniel Hurst Photography*

▶ A section of the office flooring comes from an old-growth Douglas fir tree pulled from a creek on the property. Its wood was also milled for use on the cabinetry, columns, and furniture. *Courtesy of Daniel Hurst Photography*

▲ The staggered roofline was designed for clerestory windows that spread natural light throughout the interior.
Courtesy of Daniel Hurst Photography

▲ With its long axis oriented east-west, the house is filled with the maximum amount of southern daylight throughout the year. Generous roof and canopy overhangs shade the windows during the warm summer days.
Courtesy of Daniel Hurst Photography

▲ A solar-electric system supplies most of the electricity, generating more than the house consumes annually. *Courtesy of Daniel Hurst Photography*

▲ Main living areas are arranged on one level to allow the owner to age in place. The lower level houses guests. *Courtesy of Daniel Hurst Photography*

▲ A generous patio encourages outdoor living and offers views to the vineyards below. It was constructed over a 10,000-gallon reservoir that captures rainwater for use in the vegetable and flower gardens. *Courtesy of Daniel Hurst Photography*

LEED Pilot House
Santa Monica, California
Levitt + Moss Architects

◀▲ This Southern California home has many indoor/outdoor living spaces; its entry tower allows the residents to shift back and forth between the outside and inside. After passing through the front door, a visitor enters a breezeway that offers the choice of continuing forward into a courtyard or turning and entering a guesthouse. The guesthouse is functionally separated and independent from the rest of the home and is ideal for use as a home business or apartment for an extended family member. The experience of entering the main home offers the surprise of passing through a front door into a courtyard before moving into the interior.

▲ The sun-filled kitchen opens to the family room. Countertops are made from recycled materials, and the backsplash consists of recycled glass tiles.

The 4,100-square-foot home has five bedrooms, not including the attached guesthouse. The traditionally styled stair graciously connects the first and second floors of the home. Dark stained bamboo flooring is a sustainable modern material, yet it blends seamlessly with the traditional painted millwork of the stair.

◄ One of the more unique features is the tower studio, a small, windowed room that can only be accessed from the second-floor roof deck. Evoking an adult tree house, it can be used as an exercise or work space.

LEED for Homes–Gold and Silver

LEED levels the green playing field by providing a way for all buildings claiming to be sustainable to be graded on a common scale. The certification level a building can attain is influenced, of course, by the constraints and opportunities of the wish list, site, and budget. The beauty of LEED is that it helps architects, builders, and homeowners develop a plan to lessen the impact of their building in ways that make sense for each unique project and piece of land.

CHAPTER 2

Opposite: *Courtesy of Imbue Design*

Oregon Gold
Neskowin, Oregon
Nathan Good Architects PC

▶ Most of the wood comes from an old barn on the property. Its Douglas fir was reused for roof joists, beams, columns, walls, door and window frames, flooring, cabinetry, and furniture. *Courtesy of Paula Watts Photography*

▼ Nathan Good designed the residence to withstand the Oregon coast's harsh climate, with its high winds, more than eighty inches of rain per year, and salt air. *Courtesy of Paula Watts Photography*

◀ Old wood and stone lend a lodge-like feel. Natural light is cherished in a climate dominated by overcast skies. *Courtesy of Paula Watts Photography*

◤ The barn's steel bolts and fasteners reappear as cabinet pulls, towel bars, coat hooks, and toilet paper holders. The porcelain sink and faucets came from a school; the sink is roomy enough for the children to brush their teeth at the same time. *Courtesy of Paula Watts Photography*

▲ Salvaged wood cabinets and drawer pulls support the custom sink bowl and abalone shell soap dish. *Courtesy of Paula Watts Photography*

Cape Gold
Orleans, Massachusetts
Cape Associates

▶ The entryway's staircase leads to a second-story balcony. Flooring is made of cork and bamboo, and low-VOC paints are from Benjamin Moore. In addition to LEED-Gold, this home also received NAHBGreen-Gold and Energy Star certification. *Courtesy of Roe Osborn Photography*

▲ Cape Cod's natural beauty flourishes, thanks to strategic site planning that left forty percent of the property untouched. The 2,432-square-foot house is clad in locally produced, stained white-cedar shingles, the Andersen windows have low-E glass, and the front door was handcrafted by Rogue Valley Doors. *Courtesy of Roe Osborn Photography*

▲ The Sharp solar electric system produces enough electricity to supply most of the home's energy needs.
Courtesy of Roe Osborn Photography

▲ At the heart of the home is a spacious kitchen. The bar counter is made of recycled glass from EnviroGlass, and the Candlelight Cabinetry is made with low-formaldehyde plywood. Rooftop solar panels and a Buderus boiler supply hot water. *Courtesy of Roe Osborn Photography*

Architect's Home
Saratoga, California
Srusti Architects

▲ When designing his own home, Hari Sripadanna, of Srustic Architects, focused on the professional responsibility of "walking the walk." His intent was to marry creative design with sustainable building systems and practices.

▲ His appreciation for midcentury modern design and the neighborhood context guided the design, as did the existing house's footprint and roof form. Tapping into passive solar opportunities, Sripadanna oriented the long side of the 2,732-square-foot building along an east-west axis and converted the existing gable roof into a shed roof to bring in more sunlight. To prevent summer heat gain, he calculated the sunshade depth based on the angle of the winter and summer sun.

▲ The warm, pleasant living environment is a result of daylighting and natural materials such as bamboo flooring and reclaimed redwood framing. The tall shed roof is oriented south with clerestory windows, and a contiguous interior helps to create a chimney effect: The building draws cool air from the first-floor windows and exhausts hot air through the high clerestory windows of the north-facing roof, eliminating the need for mechanical air conditioning in the mild California climate.

▶ Varying roof and ceiling heights lend intimacy to individual spaces. Synergy is the key to achieving cost-effective sustainability goals. For example, ample insulation improved the efficiency of the radiant heating system. The radiant heating system eliminated the need for attic space in which to house mechanicals and ductwork. And the clerestory windows keep the house warm in the winter and cool in the summer. These simple systems add up to more than the sum of their parts.

▲ An accent wall clad with reclaimed redwood runs through the building, tying the old footprint with the new addition on the south side.

Gold-Standard Renovation
Newport, Rhode Island
A4 Architecture + Planning

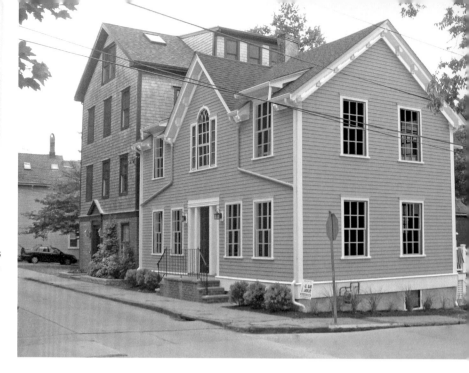

▶ A young couple asked Ross Cann to bring the house up to twenty-first-century standards.

▼ Built in 1930 in the densely occupied neighborhood between Thames and Spring Streets in Newport this small house (with central gable) was built on a rubble foundation with little to no insulation and one and a half stories, with no windows facing the east. The house had been staring into the back wall of The Elms mansion for more than eighty years without ever getting a glimpse over it.

▲ The contractor, Atlantic Building, worked with the architect and homeowner to strategize the best ways to earn LEED points. The new house is erected on the footprint of the former structure with high R-value wall insulation and ductwork that was protected from dust and other contamination during construction. Although the massing of the new house drew its cues from the Victorian-era structures nearby, all of the component parts of the new building were selected to be as energy efficient, environmentally sustainable, and long lasting as possible.

▲ The renovated house, with its two master bedrooms and two additional bedrooms, added only 600 square feet to the existing 1,200 square feet, well within LEED guidelines for an appropriately sized house.

▲ Although the project gained no additional points for improving the view, the master bedroom no longer looks at a blank wall but into The Elms gardens.

▲ The architect added a small guest suite on the footprint of a former one-story garage, with an ICF foundation and spray-foam insulated walls.

Point Crisp
Sarasota Bay, Florida
MyGreenBuilding

▶ Large balconies and overhangs soak up the southern exposure.
Photo by Detlev von Kessel

▼ Designed by Mark Sultana of DSDG and built by Stephen Ellis of MyGreenBuilding (MGB), this house is situated on a peninsula on the pristine waters of Sarasota Bay. The 1,800-square-foot home was designed for views in every direction, including from the master closet and garage. *Photo by Detlev von Kessel*

▲ On the north, an entry stair ascends through a series of semi-circular planter beds. Guest parking near the path to the front door is paved with cellular permeable pavers that provide a stable platform for vehicles while allowing storm water to percolate down into the ground. *Photo by Detlev von Kessel*

▲ Accordian doors allow the main living room to spill out onto the terraced exterior lounge and outdoor kitchen. The interplay between the interior and exterior makes it a great home for entertaining. *Photo by Detlev von Kessel*

▲ The outdoor lounge is perched above an in-ground pool fed by a cascading waterfall. A deep overhanging roof shades the southern exposure. *Photo by Detlev von Kessel*

▲ Visible in the ceiling at left, a structural glass floor inside the second-story balcony and family room filters light to the living room below. Linear diffusors on the registers evenly distribute air conditioning. *Photo by Detlev von Kessel*

◀ With three spacious interior living/family rooms for lounging, family play, and entertaining, the bedrooms didn't need to be large. However, all four bedrooms have sweeping views, outside balconies, and in-suite private baths. *Photo by Detlev von Kessel*

▼ A glass tower on the north enhances the effect of the sculptural staircase and clear tubular pneumatic elevator. The northern exposure provides great daylight without the heat. The high-performance glass is thermally insulated, low emissivity (low-E), and laminated for hurricane resistance. *Photo by Detlev von Kessel*

Hidden Gold
Orleans, Massachusetts
ZeroEnergy Design

◢ Hidden away on a sandy Cape Cod road, this 2,000-square-foot home includes three bedrooms and two full bathrooms. Its modern exterior is composed of three forms delineated by geometry, use, and material. The Red Box contains daily living spaces; the Orange Box houses guest areas; and the Cedar Box houses the private away room, master suite, and study. The site's autumnal color palette inspired the vibrant red and orange facade colors, while the Cape Cod location dictated shiplap cedar siding. *Courtesy of Michael J. Lee Photography*

◥ The homeowner's love of birdwatching inspired the second-floor roof deck. It contains a roof garden at eye level when seated, an outdoor kitchen and grill, and unobstructed views of the surrounding treetops for bird watching. *Courtesy of Michael J. Lee Photography*

▲ LEED points came from the green roof, airtight building envelope, high-efficiency condensing boiler with radiant floor heating, an allergen filtration system, a heat recovery ventilator for indoor air quality, and photovoltaic panels, which offset half of the home's electricity use. These collective efforts mean the home uses sixty percent less energy than a code-built equivalent home. The house won PRISM Award Gold | Most Innovative Green Design and Perspective in Design | Best New Construction in 2011. *Courtesy of Michael J. Lee Photography*

▲ Custom kitchen cabinetry is stained to match the homeowner's heirloom furniture and includes a built-in wine rack. Open shelves inspired by Julia Child's kitchen maximize functionality. At the tulip dining table, a cork shade with LEDs illuminates evening meals. *Courtesy of Michael J. Lee Photography*

▲ Inside, the open living space provides extensive natural lighting and views. The heavily trafficked path from the home's front entrance to the lake in the rear is tiled for durability, while the living, kitchen, and dining spaces share rapidly renewable bamboo flooring. *Courtesy of Michael J. Lee Photography*

Multigenerational
Silver

Cache Valley, Utah
AMD Architecture

This LEED-Silver home is located on the east bench of Cache Valley, Utah, with access to a local university, historic downtown, and open space trail system. It is oriented to optimize tremendous views, outdoor living, and solar strategies. The design accommodates 4,363 square feet of multigenerational living under one roof, while providing ample space for privacy. By incorporating universal design standards in all living areas, the design will meet the owner's needs well into the future. *Courtesy of Imbue Design*

▲▶ Neutral colors and materials blend into the surrounding natural landscape. Appropriately scaled forms and masses create a variety of indoor/outdoor living spaces. Patios and decks wrap the home; the decking is a highly durable recycled composite product. Site disturbance was kept to a minimum, and the site was re-vegetated with native, drought-tolerant species. *Courtesy of Imbue Design*

▲ A craftsman aesthetic inspired the locally sourced timbers, stone, and other materials used throughout. South-facing windows have permanent awnings to control passive solar gain while allowing for expansive, highly insulated glazed areas. The photovoltaic system was installed on the garage roof, which sits in full sun and allows easy maintenance access. Outdoor living areas extend from all major areas of the home into the desert setting. *Courtesy of Imbue Design*

▲ Light shelves along perimeter walls distribute indirect sunlight evenly. They also hold LED accent lights, a unifying element. The sun is the primary light source throughout the house; strategically placed insulated glazing controls solar gain and views. *Courtesy of Imbue Design*

▶ The locally made cabinetry contains no formaldehyde. Appliances are Energy Star certified, and fixtures are water-efficient. A solar thermal system circulates hot water through insulated piping to reduce heat loss. *Courtesy of Imbue Design*

▼▶ Well-placed windows and ceiling fans eliminated the need for mechanical air conditioning. A micro-zoned in-floor radiant heating system uses energy efficiently, while a heat recovery ventilator circulates fresh air when the house is closed tight in the wintertime. *Courtesy of Imbue Design*

Renovated Carriage House

Providence, Rhode Island
A4 Architecture + Planning

▶ For nearly a hundred years, this carriage house served one of the large Victorian-era homes in a neighborhood adjacent to Brown University. Over the years, the simple structure deteriorated, and eventually the university purchased it for storage. Later, it was redesigned and rehabilitated to house a senior faculty member.

▼ Although only a small amount of the material could be saved, the university wanted the house to retain its original character, and the purchasing faculty member wanted it to be as sustainable and energy efficient as possible. Although the renovated exterior would take on the character and shape of the original building in most respects, the interior had to be clean and contemporary to suit the owners' tastes and modern art collection.

◤▲ The owners joke that the house, which earned LEED-Silver, can be heated with a candle and cooled with an ice cube.

▲ To honor its history, A4 Architecture envisioned a concrete floor like the one in the original carriage house, but polished like an art gallery floor and heated and cooled by a geothermal heat pump. The walls have a special multilayer framing system to prevent thermal bridging and create a continuous airtight structure.

Sustainable Urban Villa
Cambridge, Massachusetts
Wolf Architects

▼ Designed by Wolf Architects, this LEED-Silver single family home in Cambridge, Massachusetts, is close to shops, restaurants, and public transportation. Located on a miniscule lot, the house features planters, green roofs, decks, and an inviting garden, creating a pleasant "green" retreat in the city. A geothermal well supports the heating and air conditioning systems, while photovoltaic cells on the highest roof reduce power requirements. The exterior siding was milled from recycled lumber, originally harvested as much as a century ago; reusing this material gives it new life and is durable than most contemporary siding. The National Association of Home Builders Best in American Living Awards program recognized this house with two awards: Best in Green Remodeling and Best in the North Atlantic Region. The project also won First Runner Up in the Excellence in Design Award program sponsored by *Environmental Design + Construction* and was included in the LEED Showcase of the Massachusetts USGBC. *Courtesy of Eric Roth*

◤ A green wall with shade-loving plants defines the entry court, leading to the south-facing vestibule with cobalt blue ceramic tile glazing. Paving on the court and drive combines cut New York bluestone and pea gravel, making this space into a multi-use outdoor room with a permeable surface that reduces storm water run-off. Water from the roofs is directed to underground storage recharger chambers. Grasses, trees, and shrubs in planters at both levels enhance the woodland feel. *Courtesy of Eric Roth*

◄ A birch-bark-clad column in the entry vestibule echoes the birches outdoors and introduces the natural theme inside the house. South-facing windows welcome sunlight and provide passive solar warmth for the marble flooring. The ribbed glazing maintains the owners' privacy. Built-in benches with a storage cabinet and shelf provide convenient places to sit and remove shoes or boots. This practice contributes to the home's cleanliness and indoor air quality by keeping dirt and particulates from entering the building. *Courtesy of Eric Roth*

▲ The open main level features heart pine flooring milled from reclaimed lumber, with boards as long as sixteen feet. A single oversized slab of Vermont marble clads the wall of the fireplace, which draws its combustion air from outdoors. The owners are able to easily configure the space for different activities by rearranging the sliding screens at several locations on this floor. In another poetic expression of the link between inside and outside, the screens' cutouts are derived from the leaves of neighborhood trees, while their vertical veneer stripes evoke the tree trunks outside the windows. *Courtesy of Eric Roth*

▶ On the top level, the study overlooks a roof deck, green roofs on three sides, and treetops all around. Inside, cherry cabinets and marble countertops provide natural finishes, along with the heart pine floor. Adjustable light fixtures use low-energy LEDs. Double-paned windows feature argon gas and low-E treatment for energy efficiency. The south-facing stair that connects all floors reaches this fourth-floor study and the adjoining deck. The house also has a residential elevator that will enable the owners to age in place. *Courtesy of Eric Roth*

▼ The roof deck looks out over the green roof and surrounding trees. The roof consists of a naturalistic mix of wildflower and meadow plantings, as seen in this autumn view. Striped retractable awnings on the deck off the owners' suite allow them to sit outside comfortably in a variety of weather conditions. Beyond the green roof, the chimney top rises as an abstract sculpture. On the cedar-clad side wall are light fixtures for enjoying the deck after dark, and a safety hook for servicing the green roof. Photovoltaic panels are mounted on the roof above. *Courtesy of Eric Roth*

▲ In the garden, a meditation hut with a green roof offers a quiet, sheltered spot adjacent to one of the property's pools. An undulating water course, sculpted in Corten steel by Richard Duca, winds through the site from the upper to the lower level. The gentle sounds of falling water, recycled from rainfall, contribute to the peaceful quality of this villa retreat within the city. Julie Moir Messervy Design Studio designed the sustainable landscape. Her inviting garden makes the most of this small lot and used earth-friendly practices and native plants to complement Wolf Architects' design for this LEED-Silver project. *Courtesy of Eric Roth*

Building on Principle

The field of sustainable home design can be quite confusing for the novice and sometimes even for experts. A review of the terms is helpful in sorting through the growing amount of information we are receiving about how to make our homes and lives more environmentally sustainable. First of all, what does sustainable mean? The United Nations in 1987 defined sustainability as "that which meets the needs of the present without compromising the ability of future generations to meet their own needs."

According to the US Office of the Environmental Executive (OFEE), green building is: 1) increasing the efficiency with which buildings and their sites use energy, water, and materials, and 2) reducing building impacts on human health and the environment by better siting, design, construction, operations, maintenance and removal—the complete building cycle. ("The Federal Commitment to Green Buildings: Experiences and Expectations," September 18, 2003)

The terms "green" and "sustainable" are thus the same and used interchangeably. Homeowners, designers, and builders can explore green building products and techniques and assimilate them into their projects with relative ease. Products such as low-VOC (volatile organic compound) paints are now readily available and reduce the potential for indoor air pollution that can cause illness. The Forest Stewardship Council (FSC) label assures consumers that forests have not been harmed through the harvesting of these particular wood products. WaterSense-labeled plumbing fixtures and Energy Star-labeled appliances and lighting fixtures tell the consumer that these products use less water and energy than comparable items. Experts specializing in green homes can offer suggestions for maximizing energy efficiency without increasing costs through the selection of materials and design features.

A wise consumer will look at the project's long-term costs rather than just the up-front investment. A home that reduces a power bill by ninety percent will save the homeowner thousands of dollars over the life of the home, more than offsetting its sticker price. The bottom line for our global community is that reduced energy and material consumption yields long-term gains for us all.

—Virge Temme

Hermosa Beach House

Hermosa Beach, California
Robert Nebolon Architects

▼ The Hermosa Beach house won a 2008 Grand Award from the Concrete Masonry Association of California and Nevada and the AIA California Council for its energy and resource efficiency. The jury commented: "This playful home is thirty-six percent more energy efficient than California's tough standards. Energy efficiency is achieved with shading, high performance windows, orientation, and thermal stack ventilation. Masonry provides color and texture on the ground floor and a sturdy base for the wood, steel, and glass structure above. Materials are chosen to be durable and recyclable (some are salvaged)." *Courtesy of David Duncan Livingston Photography*

▲ This "upside down" house contains the main spaces on the top floor and a garage at ground level, with the bedrooms sandwiched between—a strategy that keeps the building cool. Materials are durable, low-maintenance, and resist the salty marine air. Galvanized steel siding with a forty-year paint finish wraps the south and west elevations where the sun and wind are the harshest. Foil-coated plywood and heavily insulated walls reduce heat gain. *Courtesy of David Duncan Livingston Photography*

▲ The main entrance, at the side of the house, is well marked by brightly colored glazed concrete blocks reminiscent of the beach towels and bathing suits at the beach only a block away. An outdoor shower provides a place to rinse off after a dip in the ocean. The shaded stone and concrete act as a cooling thermal mass. *Courtesy of David Duncan Livingston Photography*

▲ The luminous main stair appears to float, with daylight streaming in from above and through the huge polycarbonate window. The stair acts as a chimney that cools the entire house. Warm air exits through a thermostatically operated skylight at the top of the stair. *Courtesy of David Duncan Livingston Photography*

◀ The teak kitchen is tucked under the roof terrace; a door leads to the roof terrace. Built-ins, such as the shelving and kitchen bar, help the small house live large. *Courtesy of David Duncan Livingston Photography*

▲ Occupying the entire top floor, the great room is open to ocean views and cooling breezes. Built-in teak cabinets were salvaged from other projects. Light enters from unexpected places, such as the fireplace shelves. *Courtesy of David Duncan Livingston Photography*

Deep Energy Retrofit
Hineberg, Vermont
Pill-Maharam Architects

▼ The owners of this 1970s split-level home initially planned to replace the windows, add insulation, and renovate the kitchen and entry. The project evolved into a gut rehab resulting in a high-performance home. *Courtesy of Susan Teare Photography*

▶ The three formerly separated levels now read as one bright, fluid living space. This is the view from the foyer to the kitchen beyond. *Courtesy of Susan Teare Photography*

▲ The new kitchen and sitting room shows the transformation of an inefficient 1970s ranch house to a more functional and environmentally friendly dwelling. *Courtesy of Susan Teare Photography*

▶ Builder, architect, and owner collaborated to develop the envelope details for the best possible performance given the existing structural limitations and budget. The construction crew excavated around the entire perimeter down to the footings and applied a continuous four-inch layer of rigid insulation from the footings to the eaves, adding an additional R-26 to the R-11 walls. Using the shallow truss bays available for insulating at the existing roof eaves, they sprayed closed-cell polyurethane foam into the existing walls through a slot in the ceiling below. After carefully air sealing the entire ceiling, they added a layer of R-60 cellulose to the existing attic and fresh air intakes for the wood stove, fireplace, and dryer. The firm detailed new window frames for

optimal air sealing. As a result, the 2,500-square-foot house achieved a low pre-drywall blower door result of 500 cfm50. To the tightened house, the team added a heat recovery ventilator. By replacing the old greenhouse attachment with efficient windows and pouring a new four-inch insulated concrete slab, the team made use of the only passive solar gain available. *Courtesy of Susan Teare Photography*

West Hollywood Bungalow

West Hollywood, California
Sarah Barnard Design

▼ Interior designer Sarah Barnard transformed a dilapidated 1918 bungalow to a bright, open, and eco-friendly space. Her remodel of this historic building made it harmonious with the owner's contemporary lifestyle and reduced its carbon footprint. *Courtesy of Chas Metivier Photography*

▶ Opening up the space between the kitchen and dining room improved daylighting. The bungalow was redone with low and no-VOC finishes, Energy Star fixtures, and a collection of vintage and antique furnishings. *Courtesy of Chas Metivier Photography*

▲ Playing on the bungalow's historic features, most of the home's furnishings were salvaged or purchased from thrift stores, which substantially reduced the amount of energy required to complete the project and contributed to the indoor air quality. Floors are made of durable, rapidly renewable bamboo. *Courtesy of Chas Metivier Photography*

▲ Eco-friendly materials echo the owner's love for natural things; the kitchen counter is made from recycled beer bottles, and the light fixtures are recycled cardboard fitted with LED fixtures. *Courtesy of Chas Metivier Photography*

▲ The hall closet was repurposed as a compact guest bathroom that uses just a few materials selected for their green attributes. Ceramic tiles, for example, require little energy to produce and can last many years with minimal maintenance. *Courtesy of Chas Metivier Photography*

▲ This Earthcraft-certified home has a simple metal roof that accentuates its modern lines. A four-foot overhang shades the living room windows toward the rear.

▲ The Nichiha lapped siding and fiber-cement rainscreen were locally manufactured and contain high levels of recycled content.

▲ The owner's extreme sensitivity to environmental toxins led to the choice of ROMA Eco-Sustainable Building Technologies for zero-VOC mineral-based paints and extremely low-VOC polyurethane and varnish.

▲ Shaded west-facing 8×8-foot sliding glass doors provide natural ventilation into the vaulted living room, while the large south-facing clerestory windows create good daylighting. The slate tile on the fireplace surround by Realstone Systems is made from leftover quarry scraps glued into panels using formaldehyde-free adhesives.

◤ The kitchen island is made from local reclaimed heart pine. Cabinets feature formaldehyde-free plywood and low-VOC finishes and adhesives. Quartz countertops provide durability and longevity, and lighting comes from LEDs.

▶ The master bathroom has a vaulted ceiling section with two north-facing skylights, bringing in ample daylight while maintaining privacy. The plumbing fixtures are low-flow, and the custom vanity is made with formaldehyde-free plywood and a low-VOC stain.

Green Residence
on a Narrow Lot

Los Angeles

Kevin Oreck | Architect

▲ Kevin Oreck designed this
1,517-square-foot house for a young
couple with a limited budget and a lot
thirty-nine feet wide. Solar panels
mounted on the large, south-facing roof
provide hot water for household use and
the radiant-heated concrete floors.
Windows were located to provide light
and views of the gardens without
compromising privacy from the adjacent
houses.

▶ The entry is tucked to the side under a
sheltering roof overhang. Exterior
materials are simple and durable: stucco
and corrugated Galvalume®. Neither
requires painting.

▲ Interior materials consist of budget-friendly drywall and maple multi-ply plywood. Because the house was designed to provide cross-ventilation, there was no need for air conditioning. The band of high windows to the right provides northern light and a private view of the sky and treetops. The windows also indirectly light the rooms on the north side of the house.

▲ The living room has a large bank of windows opening onto the lush front-yard landscaping.

▲ A high window offers privacy in the bedroom. Because there is no attic and floor space was so limited, the water heater and solar storage tank are housed in a small room above the master bath, behind the wall of cabinetry in the master bedroom.

▶ The windows of the master bedroom look into the garden and the painting studio, which screens an apartment building from view.

Cattail Cottage

Lake Bomoseen, Vermont

LineSync Architecture

▶ A zoning restriction inspired the angled bay window—the home's most prominent feature. The original L-shaped cabin could not be "squared out"; instead, the addition had to fit within the diagonal between legs of the L. By bridging the L with an angled bay window, Cattail Cottage gained a commanding view without adding foundation to the sensitive site. The interior window seat adds scale to the window wall and completes the conversation circle in the living room within a minimal space. *Courtesy of Carolyn Bates Photography and Gary Hall Photo*

▼▶ Cattail Cottage is an efficient "not so big" home of just less than 1,000 square feet. Reclamation, reuse, and restrictions literally shaped the project. The challenge was to fit a full two-bedroom home on the tight footprint of an existing summer cabin. *Courtesy of Carolyn Bates Photography and Gary Hall Photo*

The efficient kitchen provides ample storage and working space, yet feels light and uncluttered. Recessed drawers at the cabinet kick make good use of a traditionally wasted space. Single-pane windows from the original cottage were reused as kitchen cabinet doors. The builder sourced the natural-edge wood bar and heavy wood beam locally. Accessed by ladder, the loft provides a writing perch, allowing the modest rooms below to remain bright and open. *Courtesy of Carolyn Bates Photography and Gary Hall Photo*

▶ High ceilings and lofted storage add breathing room to the compact home. The open design allows for long interior views and easy entertaining. The loft above the kitchen provides scaled intimacy and an escape perch while the similarly angled window wall embraces the lake beyond. *Courtesy of Carolyn Bates Photography and Gary Hall Photo*

Cattail Cottage

◀ Windows facing the road were strategically minimized to provide privacy. A local-artisan-made concrete shelf with utility niches supports a continuous mirror stretching into the tub shower. A local metalsmith made the custom sinks in the bathroom and kitchen from a single sheet of zinc, in a tradition inspired by local Vermont farm sinks. Efficient fixtures and LED lighting completes the low-maintenance bathroom. *Courtesy of Carolyn Bates Photography and Gary Hall Photo*

123

Co-Housing
Community
Coastal Southern Maine
Richard Renner | Architects

▶ A progressive zoning ordinance made possible the construction of a clustered, zero-lot-line subdivision with the requirement that forty percent of the land remain open. The compact site plan ensured that eighty percent of the property will remain undisturbed. The main building is a unified composition of three homes and a commons, where shared functions include a place to meet (complete with kitchen and dining), library, media room, workout room, art studio, roof deck with kitchen garden, central garage, and an apartment for a future caregiver. The separate guesthouse has a living area, bedrooms, and a basement playroom. *Courtesy of Peter Vanderwarker*

▼ On a beautiful property that could have been subdivided and smothered by five freestanding houses, three couples created a cooperative community that offers them a social outlet, privacy, the prospect of aging in place, and the opportunity to enjoy and preserve a singular property and its iconic view. The owners requested individual units connected internally to a commons, along with a separate guesthouse for visiting family and friends, and business meetings and conferences. Important goals for the project included fostering interaction between the residents, energy efficiency, universal access, and durable, low maintenance materials. This project won an award from North American Copper in Architecture (NACIA), 2014. *Courtesy of Peter Vanderwarker*

▲ The building's form maximizes opportunities for daylighting, natural ventilation, and solar collectors. Solar-shading devices and deep copper eaves reduce heat gain. "Chimneys" gather the mechanical intakes and exhausts, reducing penetrations and defining individual units. Vegetated roofs retain runoff and an appealing view. Exterior walls are clad in low-maintenance, locally available cedar shingles. Low-VOC materials, water-efficient plumbing fixtures, and energy-efficient appliances were used throughout the interior. *Courtesy of Peter Vanderwarker*

▲ In the main building, the accessible entrance hallway connects the individual units and commons and organizes the plan. The design preserves individual privacy while encouraging interaction. Each living unit is, or can be made, handicap-accessible: one unit is on a single level, another has a stair wide enough for a future lift, and the third has stacked storage closets for easy conversion to an elevator. An elevator makes the commons' three floors accessible. *Courtesy of Peter Vanderwarker*

▲ In a recent publication, one of the three owners summed up the essence of this project: "Why do any of us choose to live with another human being? In marriage, partnership, and friendship, the reasons vary and are not so simple. Our arrangement is just a later-in-life experiential elaboration of that more widely experienced choice. For me, there is just more life, more growth, and more laughter than was I to live alone or with only my couple relationship." *Courtesy of Peter Vanderwarker*

A central wood pellet boiler and solar hot water collector provide heat and domestic hot water to all units, including the separate guesthouse. Overall energy use was tracked during the first twelve months of occupancy. Of the 25.6 kBtu/SF/yr. total energy used, 23.4 kBtu/SF/yr., or ninety-one percent, is from wood pellets, a local and largely renewable energy source. A 25-kilowatt PV system was also installed, with ample roof area available for additional panels in the future. The energy consumption numbers show that net zero is well within reach. *Courtesy of Peter Vanderwarker*

Floating House
San Francisco
Robert Nebolon Architects

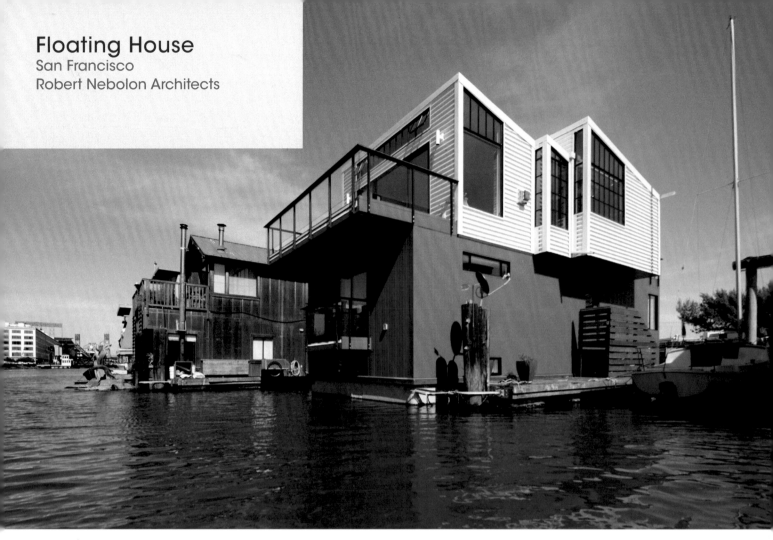

▲ For this "floating" house, Robert Nebelon Architects specified materials with high durability, low maintenance, and resistance to the salty marine air. The effect is that of a "mod" cargo container. White metal siding wraps the main floor. The sawtooth roof forms and industrial-pane windows recall the area's industrial buildings. The sawtooth design also allowed photovoltaic panels to be installed facing south. *Courtesy of Matthew Millman Photography*

▶ The main stair is designed so that daylight and fresh air enter all levels of the house, and is painted the same "International Orange" color of the nearby iconic Golden Gate Bridge. The treads are pre-engineered birch wood. *Courtesy of Matthew Millman Photography*

◄ Offering expansive San Francisco views, the teak decking is pre-fabricated and installed in a herringbone pattern. The white metal siding and roof reflects heat. *Courtesy of Matthew Millman Photography*

▼ The great room occupies the entire top level and contains the kitchen, living room, and dining room. The saw-tooth design allows high sources of daylighting and venting. Windows are brought to the ceiling so that daylight washes across the sloped ceiling. Flooring is recycled Australian cypress. *Courtesy of David Duncan Livingston*

▲ The master bathroom features daylight from surprising locations: above the sink area and low in the shower stall. Recycled live-edge teak was used for the countertop. Tile was selected from seconds at a nearby tile company. *Courtesy of Matthew Millman Photography*

◄ Large industrial-style windows flood the kitchen with light. The high clerestory windows are operable so that the house can vent naturally. All windows are double-glazed and low-E to reduce heat gain. *Courtesy of Matthew Millman Photography*

Ocean Avenue Penthouse
Santa Monica, California
Sarah Barnard Design

► Local, handmade, and unadulterated materials are the key ingredients in this contemporary Santa Monica home of 1,225 square feet. The tiny kitchen packs in both luxury and efficiency. With FSC maple hardwoods, salvaged granite slabs, LED lighting, and Energy Star rated appliances, the modest floor plan provides everything the homeowners need to cook at home. *Courtesy of Brad Nichol Photography*

▼ Salvaged live-edge woods were used to fabricate a massive living-room coffee table. Vintage elements and objects add visual interest and reduce the use of newly manufactured goods. Farrow and Ball no-VOC paint provides a seamless backdrop for high-efficiency lighting, locally made furnishings, and an art installation made of tiny, hand-thrown ceramic disks. *Courtesy of Brad Nichol Photography*

▲ Old is new again. Vintage rattan coffee table ottomans pair perfectly with a sleeper sofa from Linea and lightweight linen sheer drapery. Salvaged live-edge wood was used to fabricate custom bookshelves. Handcrafted paper wings by local artist Susan Hannon complete the space. By combining the functions of guest sleeping quarters with the high-tech requirements of entertainment, the design meets the client's needs in a modest footprint. *Courtesy of Brad Nichol Photography*

▲ The luxury master bedroom is outfitted with eco-friendly finishes in leather, rattan, maple, and wool. Repurposed case goods pair effortlessly with LED lighting, locally made organic wool carpet, and cotton draperies and bedding. The horizontal lines of the sheer drapery echo the horizon—a perfect space for the owners to welcome the morning. *Courtesy of Brad Nichol Photography*

Bungalow Transformation

Tucson, Arizona
Greener Lives LLC

▶ The tiny dining area could only have seated two people at a standard table. A custom triangular table with matching benches provides seating for four while preserving enough space for the pass-through. Greenguard-certified leather on the custom benches ensures low emissions. *Courtesy of Robin Stancliff Photography*

▶ The clients loved this 1923 bungalow and its midtown location, but the 1950s interior remodel did not fit their European sensibilities. They asked Greener Lives Interior Design to remodel the bungalow's 825-square-foot interior so they could use it as a vacation rental. *Courtesy of Mark Taylor*

▲ With four doors, two windows, a fireplace, and a built-in bookcase, there was no place for a sofa in the small living room. Converting the French doors that led to the second bedroom into a single wood door extended the living room wall, making it long enough for a sofa that folded open into a double bed and increased the home's sleeping area. Glass, metal, and leather furniture add a modern feel, and brown and beige tones warm the space. *Courtesy of Robin Stancliff Photography*

The master bedroom, like the entire house, was painted with no-VOC paint to improve indoor air quality. Converting one of the windows into a French door opened up the room and created a direct route to the new back porch and its outdoor shower. The clients added solar panels, a water harvesting system, a larger patio, and desert backyard landscaping. *Courtesy of Robin Stancliff Photography*

▲ With built-in closets for a pantry and water heater, the original kitchen was so small that the refrigerator was in the adjacent laundry room, and the washing machine was outside. Removing the wall between the kitchen and laundry room and moving the water heater outside created a kitchen/laundry room combo with a stacking washer/dryer. Cutting down the wall between the dining room and kitchen opened up the space so the galley didn't seem claustrophobic. Included are Energy Star appliances, a WaterSense faucet, energy-efficient lighting, and recycled ceramic floor tile. *Courtesy of Robin Stancliff Photography*

▲ The home's only bathroom was designed in classic 1950s style with salmon-colored tile and a built-in wood medicine cabinet. Installing a custom corner cabinet increased the floor space in this tiny bathroom, and replacing the bathtub with a glass shower made the space feel larger. A tall medicine cabinet in the corner added extra room for toiletry storage. The new bathroom includes many green features: no-VOC paint, a dual-flush toilet, WaterSense-certified fixtures, and a quartz countertop certified by Greenguard for low- to no-chemical emissions. *Courtesy of Robin Stancliff Photography*

Little Green
Wilmington, Vermont
LineSync Architecture

▼ For forty years, Little Green consisted of a single-room summer camp on a small lake in southern Vermont. At the owner's request for something resembling a New York City loft, LineSync Architecture designed a compact three-story addition, tucked gracefully into the sloping hill. *Courtesy of Kurt Johnson Photography*

The side facing the lake has a three-story space with a one-car garage on the lower level, a living room and glass porch on the main floor, and bed and bath upstairs. *Courtesy of Kurt Johnson Photography*

Ten-foot-high ceilings and exposed rafters add a sense of height and give the room a subtly urban feel. The rugged wide-plank floorboards are made of durable painted plywood. All building and finish materials in the home are non-toxic; appliances are Energy Star rated. *Courtesy of John Sprung, Sprung Photography*

▲ Ribbon windows on the long wall wrapping the stairs were designed to fit around the continuous wood frame.
Courtesy of John Sprung, Sprung Photography

◀ The bedroom is light and open to the air. *Courtesy of Kurt Johnson Photography*

▶ The owner wanted a cozy place for guests to stay—but not too long! The solution was a cozy sleeping nook that can be used for reading during the day or occasional guests. *Courtesy of John Sprung, Sprung Photography*

Hover House 3
Los Angeles
Glen Irani Architects

◀ Situated on the Venice canals in Los Angeles, Hover House 3 focuses on maximizing outdoor living on small lots by elevating the building above grade. Steel louvered panels protect the interior from excessive heat gain. Exterior wall panels create a ventilated rain screen, effectively shading and cooling the exterior walls. *Courtesy of Derek Rath*

▲ Second and third floors surround a wind scoop/sun court in anticipation of the adjacent property owner building a large home that might shade the building. The southwest-facing court promises a bright and breezy future for the house, collecting ocean breezes that cool the house and winter sun to heat it. Concrete floors throughout the 2,500-square-foot house store the sun's energy and release it at night. Hydronic loops in the floor slab exchange excessive heat with the high water table through a geothermal coil submerged in a deep pit under the garage. The court also provides much-needed space for outdoor living and children's play. *Courtesy of Derek Rath*

▶ The kitchen materials espouse two tenets: no mined or imported materials (like stone and exotic woods) and no air-polluting finishes that typically demand VOC-heavy periodic restoration. Countertops are made of Enviroseal-oiled American walnut sourced from felled, dead trees. Laminate cabinetry is constructed from no- or low-VOC locally sourced wood. *Courtesy of Derek Rath*

▶ The master bathroom, like the kitchen and other bathrooms, is designed to last indefinitely with no need for finish restoration. Cabinet faces are back-painted acrylic, as are the walls. A color change is as simple as removing the panels, sanding the backs, and spraying with no-VOC paint in any color desired. The stone is locally sourced basalt in a neutral dark gray, and all fixtures are stainless steel or Corian®. *Courtesy of Derek Rath*

▶ Fresh, bright colors make the interiors pop. *Courtesy of Derek Rath*

▲ The stair was designed as a light well, a heat chimney, and an important transitional point that greets visitors from the second floor courtyard. Climbing into the bright red space, one winds around a wall of clear structural glass suspended by steel bars from the stair tower roof. Light showers down the luminescent walls through roof tower windows positioned to vacuum air out of the house regardless of wind direction. Steel treads span from the walls to the load-bearing glass wall. *Courtesy of Derek Rath*

Sarasota Island House
Sarasota, Florida
MyGreenBuildings

▼ Stephen Ellis, CEO of MyGreenBuildings (MGB), built this house as his own vacation getaway. Its lean design of 1,870 square feet of conditioned space sleeps fourteen comfortably. *Courtesy of Gene Pollux/Pollux Photography*

▲ The home is clad in fiber-cement board-and-batten, which was repeated in some of the interior to add to its indoor-outdoor feeling. Made from reclaimed and recycled teak, the seating furniture can move inside or out and provides comfortable seating for up to forty people. The west deck seen here provides lounge seating and overlooks the private beach and azure waters leading to the Gulf of Mexico. The east deck allows views through the house to the water and features a large dining table and a game table to accommodate dinner parties. *Courtesy of Gene Pollux/Pollux Photography*

▲ The core is an open living and kitchen area thirty-two feet by eighteen feet. This space has twenty-four-foot openings of pocketing sliders on the east and west leading to screened porches (twelve feet by thirty-two feet) on both sides. When the doors are open, the space opens up to create a large pavilion, allowing the gulf breeze to pass through. With the doors closed, the views remain unobstructed. *Courtesy of Gene Pollux/Pollux Photography*

▲ The master bedroom has the requisite view to the water, light, and lots of glass.
Courtesy of Gene Pollux/Pollux Photography

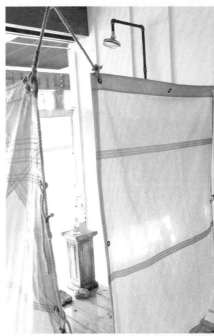

▲ To accommodate overnight visiting families, Ellis tucked in extra rooms adjoining the upper-level bedroom suites. Built into the roof structure of the large overhangs for the main floor decks, these slanted-ceiling sleeping compartments are the children's favorite. With the addition of a built-in bunk, each upper-level bedroom suite can accommodate a family of five. *Courtesy of Gene Pollux/ Pollux Photography*

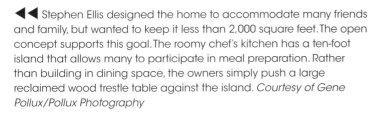

◄◄ Stephen Ellis designed the home to accommodate many friends and family, but wanted to keep it less than 2,000 square feet. The open concept supports this goal. The roomy chef's kitchen has a ten-foot island that allows many to participate in meal preparation. Rather than building in dining space, the owners simply push a large reclaimed wood trestle table against the island. *Courtesy of Gene Pollux/Pollux Photography*

▸ Ellis designed and crafted the beds from salvaged beams with a history. The master bed was fabricated from a large hand-painted beam that supported the ceiling in the once elegant Ringling Hotel (owned by the famed circus magnate) that was demolished in the 1990s. Other beds were made of old-growth heart pine salvaged from what Ellis believes was a demolished cigar factory in the historic Ibor City section of Tampa. *Courtesy of Gene Pollux/Pollux Photography*

▲ Reclaimed sails from a friend's schooner reappear as panels that enclose the outdoor shower and cover closet doors in the guest rooms. They give the space an airy feeling and remind Ellis of the origin of his design and construction philosophy. "My space-efficient design approach and connection to sustainability comes from my days living aboard and maintaining yachts in my youth with my family and as I worked through college. My construction philosophy also stems from the structural integrity of blue-water yachts and the quality of the joinery work." *Courtesy of Gene Pollux/Pollux Photography*

▲ *Courtesy of Gene Pollux/Pollux Photography*

RiverRest
Marinette, Wisconsin
Virge Temme Architecture

◄ "Have nothing in your home that you do not know to be useful or believe to be beautiful." This mandate from William Morris in 1868 guides the design of many green homes, including this small, 1,600-square-foot cottage by Virge Temme, who subcribes to the belief that a truly green home is one that is no larger than required for the homeowners' needs. Its form drew inspiration from 1940s fishing cottages: simple, iconic shapes and rustic wood siding that integrate seamlessly with the neighboring surroundings. The interior, however, offers a dramatic modern interplay of forms and volumes, belying the compact scale and fooling the eye into perceiving the diminutive rooms as something much more grand. *Courtesy of Valo Photography*

▲ Because the desirable views faced east, there was little opportunity for using southern windows to light the home. An all-white interior amplifies sunlight and bounces it back into the otherwise dim recesses. A stained high-gloss concrete floor further enhances the effect, transforming a mundane construction material into a beautiful finished surface and eliminating redundant flooring materials. *Courtesy of Valo Photography*

◄ Frank Lloyd Wright proved that manipulating ceiling heights and interior volumes elevates the senses. When one moves from low-ceilinged small spaces into taller, larger ones, the effect is amplified. In this home, an extremely low, narrow corridor runs between low-ceilinged sleeping rooms, connecting the main house with a private guest suite and dramatically expanding the perceived volume of the adjacent rooms (top left). An intimate reading loft tucked below the roofline provides a treehouse-like hideaway overlooking the living space below. It also creates a perfect place for stargazing under skylights that are part of the natural ventilation system. *Courtesy of Valo Photography*

▲ Designing compact spaces includes the thoughtful use of built-in furnishings. Children's beds are integrated within storage drawers and shelves. Elsewhere, wooden shelving inserted into dead space behind the fireplace serves as night stands in the master bedroom. Laundry, mechanical equipment, and storage for sports paraphernalia hide behind a colonnade of French doors, transforming a utilitarian mudroom into a bright, inviting retreat. *Courtesy of Valo Photography*

◄ In keeping with the leisurely lifestyle of summer cottages, landscaping is composed simply of no-mow grasses. Even the driveway is a grassy strip stabilized by a geo-grid. The siding is locally harvested stained cedar. A three-season porch with interchangeable screen and glass panels on the southeast corner offers warm respite on brisk autumn days, and breezes draw from this end of the house northward through loft skylights, cooling the home on summer nights. *Courtesy of Valo Photography*

▲ Locally sourced cabinetry is built from sustainably harvested woods. Appliances, lighting, and plumbing fixtures were selected for their low energy and water usage. To reduce energy needs, exterior walls filled with open-cell foam insulation were built by staggering 2×4 studs along five-and-one-half-inch-wide top and bottom plates, thus reducing thermal bridging. The vaulted roof was also filled with water-based open-cell foam, which lends higher R-values per inch than other insulation types. *Courtesy of Valo Photography*

Prefabricated Green
Vashon Island, Washington
Chester Architecture

▶ Vashon Island does not have a storm water system, other than the ditches and gutters that carry untreated storm water runoff to Puget Sound. This 2,100-square-foot house collects the water from roofs, driveways, and other impervious surfaces and transfers it through bio-swales and piping to an infiltration trench downstream from the house. The trench can fill and overflow, allowing the water to sheet flow over a meadow before leaving the property. This system absorbs and removes contaminants and helps to protect neighbors and Puget Sound from pollutants and water damage. *Courtesy ©Keith Brofsky*

▼ This unique residence's panelized and prefabricated systems helped it earn Built Green (a Washington state certification program) and LEED points. A repurposed silo contains the dining room. The inside is furred with wood studs and insulated to R-38 in both walls and ceilings. *Courtesy ©Keith Brofsky*

▲ The custom home was made in a factory that uses computer modeling to panelize virtually any design. The panelized system uses forty percent fewer labor hours to construct, has fifty-five percent less lumber waste, sixty percent less sheeting waste, and uses roughly two percent less lumber and sheathing than conventional stick framing. Waste materials at the factory are recycled. *Courtesy ©Keith Brofsky*

▲ The manufacturer supplied wall panels, insulation, windows, interior and exterior doors, siding, roofing, and hardware. General contractor Jim Lyman added mechanical and electrical systems, gypsum board, and finishes. The four-inch concrete slab-on-grade floor system has a hard-troweled and sealed finish and was insulated to R-30. The hydronic radiant-floor heating system is powered by a ninety-eight-percent efficient electric boiler little bigger than a two-quart thermos. *Courtesy ©Keith Brofsky*

▲ The hydronic floor heating system is zoned so that bathrooms can be warmer and bedrooms cooler than the rest of the house. The bath looks out on a private zen garden accessed from the shower area through sliding doors. Shoji screens provide additional privacy. The shower and tub room is designed as a wet area with a floor drain. The home also has a gravity-fed drainfield septic system. *Courtesy ©Keith Brofsky*

◀ Engineered, prefinished wood flooring softens the impact of concrete in the main circulation spaces. Exterior glass doors and windows are extruded, argon-filled fiberglass insulated for maximum thermal resistance. *Courtesy ©Keith Brofsky*

◀ Bork Design created this modern Earthcraft-certified home for the Athens Land Trust, a local non-profit promoting land conservation and affordable subsidized housing. The building's long street frontage is a contemporary adaptation of the 1950s ranch houses prevalent in the neighborhood. Slight cantilevered volumes on three sides, like the cedar rain screen shown here, give the facade some relief. The shed roof directs water away from the 1,500-square-foot house and accommodates a vaulted ceiling over the open living area with clerestory windows facing the street.

◤ The rectangular building envelope and stacked bathrooms—which allows for a simple plumbing run—kept the construction efficient. Nichiha lapped and board-and-batten fiber-cement siding contains recycled content and is made in Georgia.

▲ Deep roof overhangs and trellised awnings shade the ample glazing. The cedar siding is applied as a rain screen with an air cavity behind that allows the material to dry out after a rain, thereby improving its longevity.

▲ Framing and decking are made of local southern pine. An open carport disperses exhaust pollutants.

▲ The custom-designed polycarbonate stair window has a ribbed surface and cavity filled with air—a more economical choice than a large window.

◀ South-facing windows on the front elevation were built on site using glazing panels with a high insulation value. The overhangs protect against heat gain. High ceilings not only make a small home feel larger, they also keep interiors cool in hot southern climates.

Chapter 4. Passive House Standards

Passive House is a design methodology and energy standard that can result in a super-insulated, airtight building that uses seventy to ninety percent less energy for heating and cooling than a conventional building. A popular methodology in Europe, particularly in Germany, it is a fledging movement in the United States, where the Passive House Institute US describes it as "the most rigorous building energy standard in the world."

A certified Passive House must meet stringent energy and airtightness requirements. The overall heating load may not be more than 4.75 kTBtu per square foot per year, and the overall energy load must be no more than 3.79×10^4 btu/ft^2 per year. Air leakage through gaps in the house must be less than 0.6 air changes per hour when tested at 50 Pascals of pressure using a blower-door test. Passive Houses rely on proper solar orientation, an airtight building envelope, mechanical fresh-air ventilation, and the reuse of waste heat to meet the certification requirements.

—Virge Temme

CHAPTER 4

Opposite: *Courtesy of Valo Photography*

Ithaca
Door County, Wisconsin
Virge Temme Architecture

▶ The owners proposed the concept, borrowed from the pages of Homer: Ithaca: a place one returns to in dreams. The epic theme resonated with Wisconsin architect Virge Temme. Together, owners and architect dreamed of a home that had the least impact on resources, yet was cozy and pleasing and could be returned to for generations. Passive House modeling earned Ithaca 112 LEED points and a Platinum rating. The 2,600-square-foot home was modeled to within eight percent of Passive House requirements. Because of the irregular roofline, the Passive House advisor suggested that if an alternative strategy was used for the modeling, the house would certainly pass. That modeling process would have taken several weeks and several thousands of dollars more to complete, plus the additional cost of registration. The owners and architect agreed that actual performance was the objective, and having met their performance goals, they chose to seek solely the LEED certification. The home's actual performance has outperformed the modeling. *Courtesy of Valo Photography*

▼ The architect specified recycled and recyclable materials throughout the house. The corrugated steel siding, steel roofing, and steel brise soleil are twelve percent recycled steel and fully recyclable at end of life. Cellulose insulation was chosen because it is environmentally inert, recycled, and sourced within 100 miles. The roof is made of sixteen-inch recycled wood I-joists. Floors and patios are locally sourced concrete. Wood, steel, and paper-based construction scrap was recycled, yielding a less than 1,200 pounds of construction waste. *Courtesy of Valo Photography*

▲ A combination of ninety-eight percent efficient air-source heat pump and an energy recovery ventilator supply most of the heating and ventilation while managing humidity levels. Supply and return air runs through sealed ductwork, WaterSense plumbing fixtures reduce the flow of water without compromising quality, and water lines are insulated. Short plumbing runs and a recirculating pump for instant hot water also conserve water. Light fixtures are Energy-Star rated and use LED and compact fluorescent bulbs. No vents or electrical boxes penetrate the roof envelope, and wall outlets are sealed to prevent heat loss. *Courtesy of Valo Photography*

▲ Sited in an ancient meadow, the house was positioned to preserve trees and enhance views, and a tight ten-foot construction perimeter was maintained around the building footprint. The construction crew also stockpiled the excavated soil to retain the meadow's seed stock, which was replanted after construction ended. Roof runoff is collected in two rain gardens, and a small vegetable garden sits just steps from the kitchen door. *Courtesy of Valo Photography*

▲ By using space creatively, the architect was able to fit sleeping rooms for eight within the house's 2,600 square feet. Here, a laundry is concealed in the passage between the master bedroom and foyer. Built-in storage cabinets run the length of the living and dining room and kitchen. Built-in daybeds on the second floor landing act as both a secondary sitting room and extra sleeping accommodations. *Courtesy of Valo Photography*

Temme used Passive House's PHPP software to calculate insulation levels and make sure all the components worked together to achieve the desired result. Ithaca was built using double-wall construction and super-insulated to R-30 below grade, R-42 walls, R-60 roof/ceiling, and R-7 exterior doors and windows. Windows were sized and placed to optimize passive solar gain, and the EPA-approved closed-combustion fireplace is used for enjoyment rather than additional heat. The fireplace's limestone veneer came from a neighboring quarry, and the kitchen flooring and cabinetry is bamboo. *Courtesy of Valo Photography*

Net Zero Energy Residence

Norwich, Vermont
Pill-Maharam Architects

▲▼ This certified Passive House contains 1,784 square feet on the first floor, 580 square feet on the second floor, and a 1,780-square-foot walkout basement. It scored 0.46 ACH50 on a blower door test. *Photos courtesy of Glenn Callahan Photography*

▲ An open plan makes the most of daylighting and the southern orientation.

◄ The building uses a ground-source heat pump with a closed loop for heating and domestic hot water, and a ground-linked pre-heating/cooling coil for the heat recovery ventilator. Metal and fiber-cement siding and metal roofing were chosen for their good looks, low maintenance, and durability.

Passive House Retreat
Little Compton, Rhode Island
ZeroEnergy Design

▼ This retreat located in a beautiful Rhode Island ocean community shows that smart things come in small packages. The sleek, simple, gable-roofed structure fulfills the family's program requirements and is designed to the Passive House standard. The resulting 1,200-square-foot home comfortably sleeps six while consuming eighty-six percent less energy compared to a similar new home built only to code requirements. It won a Design Award from Boston Society of Architects and a Grand Award from *EcoHome* magazine in 2012. *Courtesy of Greg Premru Photography*

▲ The homeowners sought a modern two-plus-bedroom private retreat, right-sized for their family of six. The site offered excellent southern exposure, paired with the challenge of a lovely north-facing agrarian view. *Courtesy of Greg Premru Photography*

▲ Simple finishes, bright colors, minimal trim, and concrete floors achieve a clean, fresh look on the interior. A central gathering space with a vaulted ceiling houses living and cooking areas and includes the flexibility of a movable kitchen island. *Courtesy of Greg Premru Photography*

▲ The airy, south-facing dining nook has built-in seating to accommodate everyday family use and larger gatherings. A combination of high-performance windows, passive solar, air sealing, and insulation reduces the heating load to a fraction of a typical home. *Courtesy of Greg Premru Photography*

◀ On the north, large triple-pane lift-and-slide doors connect the interior to a patio and views across the fields. *Courtesy of Greg Premru Photography*

▶ The gable form is a defining feature, with its iconic shape repeated inside and out. Bedrooms are located at each end of the home, with an open living space in the center. *Courtesy of Greg Premru Photography*

Prescott Passive House
Kansas City, Kansas
Studio 804

▶ The Prescott house was designed to the German Passive House standard, which seeks to lower the home's energy demand by as much as ninety percent. The design addresses affordability by providing passive strategies for sustainability, rather than using costly systems such as solar panels and wind turbines to offset energy demand.

▼ The product of eight months' work by sixteen graduate students at the University of Kansas, the 1,700-square-foot house bestows many amenities within a small ecological footprint. The FSC-certified Douglas fir siding was finished using an ancient Japanese method called *shou-sugi-ban* in which the surface is charred. This technique lends permanent UV protection to the wood while also making it insect, rot, and flame resistant. The students chose metal roofing for its recycled content, low maintenance, and affordability. The lot was finished with native drought-tolerant grasses, rain gardens, and deciduous trees to shade the house from the southwest sun. Rain runoff from the roof is diverted to a 1,000-gallon cistern.

◀ South-facing glazing allows ample light into the home, while louvers on the exterior, optimally angled to block summer sun and allow winter heat gain, cut glare and provide privacy. Window placement and white interior surfaces invite light deep into the house, eliminating the need for artificial lighting during the day. In accordance with Passive House design standards, openings on the north are non-existent to minimize heat loss.

▲ With goals ranging from material and energy efficiency to affordability and longevity, the house provides a modern answer to the often-unanswered question, "How can I live lightly?" Countertops and windowsills are made of Richlite, a recycled paper composite product.

◀ The living room's concrete slab floor provides thermal mass, reducing the need for mechanical heating in winter. The concrete contains a high percentage of fly ash to increase the recycled content.

Lake Farm
Door County, Wisconsin
Virge Temme Architecture

A thorough remodeling converted a small, rustic 1940s log cabin in Northern Wisconsin into a modern, energy-efficient retreat for large family gatherings. Although the home had optimum passive solar potential, the existing structure took no advantage of this opportunity. No insulation and a leaky envelope made the building costly to operate. The owner's dream was to increase the number of bedrooms and to bring the home as close to Passive House performance as possible. Although the 3,600-square-foot project nearly met the energy levels of Passive House for remodeled structures, it had a gambrel roof; the intersections of the roof planes each count as a corner, resulting in possibly the least efficient roof design possible. If the roof had been a simple gable, it would have met the standards. *Courtesy of Valo Photography*

The original log structure was retained and left exposed inside. Exterior log walls were left in place and expanded inward to create space for an extra twelve inches of insulation and lighten the dark interior. Painting these walls white amplified the limited natural daylighting. Locally sourced recycled barn beams and logs augment the existing log structure and provide exquisite textural finish details. Locally harvested and milled pine floors were finished with tung oil. *Courtesy of Valo Photography*

Passive House certification requires remodeled homes to achieve a 7.75 kBtuh of total energy use per square foot per year. This home originally consumed over 40. By maximizing passive solar gain and increasing insulation, the house achieved modeled energy values of 8.15. The two wings added to the south elevation to accommodate a new dining room and bedroom also provide passive solar heat throughout the first floor. Deep window wells reveal the foot-thick walls dense-packed with cellulose insulation for R-42 protection against the deep cold. Triple-pane windows are engineered for optimum solar gain. The vaulted ceiling is sixteen inches thick, providing an R-62 insulation value on the roof. *Courtesy of Valo Photography*

▲ A geothermal boiler system provides heating and cooling, and an energy recovery ventilator supplies fresh air. In-floor radiant heat assures even heating, so that temperatures can be comfortably lowered. Because of the home's tight building envelope and the owner's desire for a professionally equipped kitchen, an at-source makeup air system was installed to offset the stove's high-powered commercial exhaust fan. New airtight doors and fresh-air intake openings made the two existing masonry fireplaces more efficient. *Courtesy of Valo Photography*

▶ The dynamic contrast of old and new is especially evident in the entry gallery, where stained concrete floors and crisp white plaster collide with hand-hewn logs and stripped-bark beams. Interior plank doors from original second-floor bedrooms found new life on entry closets. A block-and-tackle hoist allows large items to be hauled upstairs through a new barn door that opens onto a viewing loft overlooking the entry gallery. In homage to the farm origins, the swinging loft gate panels are agricultural pigwire. *Courtesy of Valo Photography*

◀ While the exterior retained its original log structure, the additions are clad in cedar shingles stained to match the weathered logs. The architect specified a metal roof for its longevity, recyclable qualities, and rainwater collection benefits, and roughed in a chase for future solar electric panels. Skylights and solar tubes provide daylighting to interior second-floor rooms. The landscaping consists of no-mow grasses, drought-tolerant plantings, rain gardens, and pathways made of local flagstone and crushed stone. *Courtesy of Valo Photography*

Vermont Residence

Norwich, Vermont
Pill-Maharam Architects

▲ This Passive House takes its shape from the landscape; its compound wall and roof angles fold sculpturally into the south-facing hill. That design goal presented the challenge of how to marry complex geometry with the simple forms that optimize thermal efficiency and passive solar gain. The house is highly insulated, with R-35 on below-grade walls, R-61 above grade, and R-74 on the roof. Windows are Passive House certified, foamed and taped, and positioned for maximum daylighting. Double-stud wall framing helped to eliminate thermal bridging. Most of the insulation is cellulose, with a small amount of spray foam. The roof holds a 9-kWh photovoltaic system and the project achieved a HERS score of 2. Modeling suggests that this house should operate at net zero energy use. With a combination of Galvalume® and fiber-cement rain screen siding, this sturdy house will last for years to come.

▲ Heating demand is a low 3.81 kBtu/sf/yr., which only required one small air-source heat pump for the entire building. A special drain system extracts heat from the waste water and returns it to the hot water tank. That system, combined with low-flow showerheads and a heat pump hot water heater, helps to conserve energy and water.

Chapter 5. Natural Building Methods

Major strides have been taken to reduce the environmental impact of our housing stock. Home automation systems allow us to regulate temperature and lighting remotely to reduce power consumption. Building envelopes are super-insulated with thick barriers of polystyrene foam. LEDs reduce lighting costs, and photovoltaic panels supply electricity from the sun.

Yet there is a simple, quiet faction of green architecture that follows an ancient creed of using materials in their natural state. This is the world of straw and mud, clay and cob: what is known as alternative or natural building.

Adobe, straw bale, cob, and rammed-earth construction have been part of the building lexicon for millennia. Scattered throughout the world and across most climate zones, these homes rise up from the ground, serve their purpose, and then are assimilated back into the earth with little or no environmental impact.

Another advantage is that they are often cool in summer and warm in winter, thus reducing heating requirements and nearly eliminating the need for mechanical cooling. They are also more textural, sculptural, and organic in appearance than typical wood-frame-and-drywall homes, and as such often have a pleasing visceral effect on humans. Earth and straw bale walls are "breathable," so moisture, odors, and indoor toxins carried in the air move from the inside to the outside. And because the buildings are coated with natural pigmented clays and lime, their indoor air quality is usually superior to conventional homes, eliminating the need for automated ventilation systems. Properly maintained and protected from snow and rain, they can last as long as wood-frame homes.

The disadvantages, while not insurmountable, explain why more such homes have not caught on in the United States. First, few people know how to build them, making it difficult to estimate construction costs. Many natural homes, especially straw bale, are built with volunteer laborers who are guided by one or two experts. Except in the Southwest, where adobe construction is common, these natural building techniques are often unfamiliar to building inspectors, too. In some cases, building codes must be reviewed and revised to accommodate them.

Clays and other earthen materials must be properly selected and treated to ensure durability. Straw bales must be harvested and stored in dry conditions, or mold can result. Incorrect detailing of earthen or straw bale homes can be catastrophic, resulting in their collapse from the ground up. Exterior finishes must be maintained and reapplied regularly to keep the core materials from decomposing.

If the disadvantages can be surmounted—and usually they can—the resulting homes are harmonious structures that many believe are a solution to society's environmental disconnect and a way back to a more sustainable relationship to our Earth.

—Virge Temme

Eden Straw Bale
Wilmington, Vermont
LineSync Architecture

▶The owners visualized a solar home and medical office that could operate off the power grid and feel connected to the earth. LineSync designed a straw bale envelope that acts like an uninterrupted blanket, wrapping around the simple post-and-beam structure. Substantial roof overhangs protect the clay-coated straw bales from water. The straw bale walls are also raised off the ground on a protective stem wall faced with lakeshore stones. *Courtesy of Carolyn L. Bates Photography*

▼ Double-glazed windows puncture the walls in select locations to optimize light and views. The most prominent glazing opens onto a south-facing deck and a landscape that incorporates native plants and pervious gravel walkways. Oriented south to optimize future solar panel installation, the 3,200-square-foot building mass absorbs the winter sun, and the large eaves protect it from heat gain in summer. There are few windows on the east and west. The North East Sustainable Energy Association (NESEA) gave this home the First Place Award, Places to Live, in 2004. *Courtesy of Carolyn L. Bates Photography*

▲ Between the roof trusses are three feet of cellulose insulation made from ground newspapers mixed with borax to resist fire and rot. The protected space below is open, inviting, and energetic with natural southern light filtering in. Below is the quiet office quarters. *Courtesy of Carolyn L. Bates Photography*

▶ Details inside and out create moments of delight and provide the clients with opportunities to connect with the building. The owners completed much of the construction themselves, including hand-coating the straw bale walls with lime-based plaster. One of the owners made the stained glass window. Exterior windows are double pane with low-E coating to reduce heat gain. Local materials and landscape views root the house to the site; yet, it is also a tangible space that adapts to many uses. *Courtesy of Carolyn L. Bates Photography*

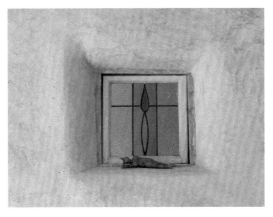

Courtyard-Style Straw Bale Residence
Borrego Springs, California
Hubbell & Hubbell Architects

▶ A sculptural wrought-iron gate and stone column set the tone for the home. *Courtesy of Mike McElhatton*

▼ This straw bale house is situated at the point where three knolls come together in the heart of the Anza-Borrego Desert. The roof steps with the slope, nestling into the site with a quiet reverence for the desert landscape. *Courtesy of Mike McElhatton*

▲ The floor plan alludes to the traditional Spanish courtyard home. Two bedroom wings enfold a south-facing patio with an outdoor fireplace shaded by a rustic wooden trellis constructed from salvaged timbers. The swimming pool and spa sit on sand-colored flagstone surrounded by native landscaping. The nature-centered design connects the owners and their guests to the desert's breathtaking beauty. The structural system is composed of wood, steel posts, and reclaimed timber beams with straw bale infill. A passive solar system heats water for the pool. Other features include a rooftop viewing deck, custom stained-glass doors and lighting features, custom mosaic tile, and custom railings and gates. *Courtesy of Mike McElhatton*

▲ Wood and stained glass entry doors create a spectacular entry for this unique home in the California desert. *Courtesy of Mike McElhatton*

▲ A desire for clear views in any direction drove the decision to design an underground four-car garage entered through a tunnel. Light flows into the garage through light wells in the curved walls and through the circular fountain's glass bottom. The underground garage also provides thermal mass for passively heating and cooling the home. *Courtesy of Mike McElhatton*

Acknowledgments

With each architecture book, I learn more about how to build a beautiful, affordable, and sustainable house with soul. My research for this book has taught me how to help the next generation and save money and the environment over the long term.

Three architects lent their expertise and wisdom to this book. Ross Cann drew on his vast experience in suggesting areas and people to consult. Adam Prince helped me understand more about LEED, and Virge Temme clarified the world of Passive Houses and natural building methods.

American National Standards Institute (ANSI) is a national nonprofit membership organization that coordinates development of national consensus standards.

Blower door test determines a building's airtightness.

Brise soleil refers to a variety of permanent sun-shading structures. Typically, a horizontal projection extends from a facade that has large amount of glass to prevent it from overheating during the summer. Often louvers are incorporated into the shade to prevent the high-angle summer sun from falling on the facade, but also to allow the low-angle winter sun to provide passive solar heating.

Build It Green is a professional, nonprofit membership organization that promotes healthy, energy- and resource-efficient buildings in California. Based in Berkeley, Build It Green offers professional training and other support services, maintains a regional green products database, and administers the Green Point Rated home certification program.

Builders Challenge is a US Department of Energy (DOE) program that promotes the construction of "better than Energy Star" homes. A home must have a maximum Home Energy Rating (HERS, see below) of 70 to meet the requirements.

Building Biology (BB) is a field of building science investigating the indoor living environment for a variety of irritants. BB looks at how a building affects occupants' health and the surrounding ecosystem. Practitioners believe the environment of residential, commercial, and public buildings can produce a restful or stressful environment.

Building envelope refers to exterior components of the outer shell of a house that provide protection from colder (and warmer) outdoor temperatures and precipitation; including the house foundation, framed exterior walls, roof or ceiling, insulation, and air sealing materials.

Canale is a short, narrow trough that protrudes through the parapet of a flat roof and directs water away from the side of a building onto the ground below. Drainage on a flat roof (or nearly flat) is very important. A minimal slope of 1:4 is needed for water to drain off the roof properly to prevent leaks and other roof problems. Canales are commonly made of wood reinforced with a metal lining. Southwestern adobe style flat roofed homes traditionally use canales instead of gutters to drain water from a flat roof.

Certified Green Professional™ (CGP) is a National Association of Home Builders designation that identifies builders and other industry professionals who incorporate green building principles into residences.

Convection basically means that air rises as it warms. In winter, we pay for the energy lost by the heat rising through the attic. During summer, the attic captures nearly all of our home's heat, requiring attic ventilation. Installing the correct thickness of insulation is absolutely necessary; attic ventilation and insulation must suit the region.

Conduction is the transfer of heat from particle to particle by the movement of fluids such as air or water. We learned in school about natural convection; i.e., hot air rises and cool air sinks. Forced convection refers to the use of fans or pumps to move a fluid/air and the heat contained in it.

Embodied energy refers to the energy required to extract and process the raw materials, manufacture the product, and transport the material and product from source to end use. Building materials with high embodied energy include asphalt, metals, glass, and petroleum-based thermoplastics used in siding, flooring, insulation, and vapor barriers. Building products with lower embodied energy include wood, wood and agricultural fiber, reused materials, and many recycled content and byproduct-based products.

Energy Star Home is a US Environmental Protection Agency program that sets benchmarks for better energy efficiency, durability, and quality than a standard home. An Energy Star certified home delivers energy-efficiency savings of up to 30 percent when compared to typical new homes.

Energy Star appliances and lighting fixtures denote products that use less water and energy than comparable items.

Forest Stewardship Council (FSC) is an independent not-for-profit organization established to promote the responsible management of the world's forests. An FSC label helps consumers make informed choices about the forest products they purchase.

Gabion walls are constructed by filling large, galvanized steel baskets with rock. Gabion baskets can be stacked in various shapes, and they conform to ground movement and drain freely. In addition to being features of residential landscape design, especially in Europe, they are commonly used to stabilize slopes or shorelines against erosion.

Geothermal heat pump (GHP) uses the earth's natural energy to both heat and cool buildings. It uses the earth as a heat source (in the winter) or a heat sink (in the summer). This design takes advantage of the moderate temperatures in the ground to boost efficiency and reduce the operational costs of heating and cooling systems. It may be combined with solar heating for even greater efficiency.

Heat Recovery Ventilator (HRV) exchanges stale air inside the home with fresher outdoor air. It is designed to provide comfort in colder climates where the house is tightly sealed. The system captures heat from the indoor air before exhausting it outdoors.

Home Energy Pros is a Lawrence Berkeley National Labs and *Home Energy Magazine* social media website. A group has formed around the Thousand Home Challenge (see entry below) on this site, where participants can share knowledge.

Home Energy Rating System (HERS) is the analysis of a home's energy efficiency. HERS rates buildings from 1–100, with 100 being a standard home built to meet current energy codes. A home with a 70 HERS rating is 30 percent more energy efficient than required by today's energy codes. A home with a 30 HERS rating is 70 percent more energy efficient. Many LEED homes are in the 20–30 HERS range.

Insulated concrete form (ICF) building blocks refer to interlocking modular units that are dry-stacked (without mortar) and filled with concrete. The forms lock together somewhat like Lego bricks and create a form for the structural walls or floors of a building. As more stringent energy efficiency and natural-disaster-resistant building codes are adopted, ICF construction has become commonplace for both low-rise commercial and high-performance residential construction.

Leadership in Energy and Environmental Design (LEED), developed by the United States Green Building Council, is a comprehensive rating system that helps architects and builders produce energy-efficient, water-conserving buildings that use sustainable resources and materials. Launched in the early 1990s, LEED is now used worldwide. Projects are evaluated according a point system, with points distributed among the following categories: Sustainable Sites (SS), Water Efficiency (WE), Energy & Atmosphere (EA), Materials & Resources (MR), Indoor Environmental Quality (IEQ), and Innovation in Design (ID).

Living Building Challenge is a rigorous performance standard administered by the International Living Future Institute. The Institute offers green building and infrastructure solutions that go from single-room renovations to neighborhoods and whole cities.

National Association of Home Builders National Green Building Program (NAHBGreen) provides builders with educational resources, advocacy tools, a credible green standard, and referrals to a national green home certification system by the Home Innovation Research Labs, an independent third party. Working with the International Code Council, NAHB spearheaded the development of the National Green Building Standard for all residential construction and renovation projects. ANSI approved this standard in 2009, making it a benchmark for green homes

Passive House, developed in Germany, is a rigorous standard for energy efficiency. Passive House-certified buildings are estimated to be about ninety percent more energy efficient than those built according to today's US energy code. They are usually so energy efficient that they do not require heating systems: body heat from the occupants, heat generated from appliances, and solar heat are often all that are needed. Because the building shell is so tight, all Passive House buildings incorporate air exchange systems to keep fresh air circulating.

Rammed earth is a method of building walls whereby a mixture of earth is compacted in layers between forms. Rammed earth walls can absorb the heat during the day and release it at night. This ancient building method has recently been revived as people seek more sustainable building materials and natural building methods. Rammed earth homes (think of the pueblo) are simple to construct, noncombustible, thermally massive, strong, and durable. They can be labor-intensive to construct without machinery and susceptible to water damage if inadequately maintained.

Structural insulated panels (SIPs) are a high-performance building system for residential and light commercial construction. SIPs consist of an insulating foam core sandwiched between two structural facings. They can be fabricated to fit nearly any building design and application, such as exterior wall, roof, floor, and foundation.

A **thermal bridge**, also called a **cold bridge**, is a junction where insulation is not continuous, causing heat loss. A thermal bridge occurs when there is a gap between materials and the structural framework, such as at the junctions of facings and floors, cross walls, and roofs, and at doors and windows.

Thermal mass is the ability of a building's mass to store and release heat, protecting it from temperature fluctuations. For example, thermal mass will absorb thermal energy when the surroundings are higher in temperature than the mass, and give thermal energy back when the surroundings are cooler.

Thousand Home Challenge (THC) is a call to reduce annual site energy consumption of existing North American homes by seventy percent or more through a combination of energy efficiency, renewable resources, community-based solutions, and behavioral choices. By redefining "deep energy reductions" and providing easily verifiable criteria, the THC provides a way to develop integrated solutions to the problems of housing affordability, durability, and sustainability.

Trombe wall is used to boost passive solar heat gain. A glass wall is typically built a few inches in front of a house's exterior, south-facing masonry wall. The sun's warmth is absorbed into the wall during the sunlit hours of winter and conducted to the interior, where it is released at night.

United States Green Building Council (USGBC) is a non-profit organization that champions environmentally friendly building through its LEED program, education and advocacy, and a national network of chapters and affiliates.

Volatile organic compound (VOC) is a substance that contains carbon and evaporates, or "off-gases," at room temperature. Paint and paint products are the second largest source of VOCs, after cars, and a major cause of "sick building syndrome." Painting and paint-stripping can increase VOC levels inside a house up to 1,000 times. High-quality low- and no-VOC paints are now readily available and reduce the potential for indoor air pollution.

WaterSense is an EPA partnership program with manufacturers, retailers, distributors, and utilities to guide consumers in purchasing high-performing, water-efficient products. WaterSense labeled products are backed by independent third-party certification and meet EPA's specifications for water efficiency and performance.

Sources

A4 Architecture and Planning
320 Thames St.
Newport, RI 02840
www.a4arch.com

AMD Architecture
11 South 900
East Suite 103
Salt Lake Ci
www.amdarchitecture.com

Bork Design
150 Pulaski Heights
Athens, GA 30601
www.bork-design.com

Brian C. Freeman Construction
136 Tierra Encantada
Corrales, NM 87048

Butler Armsden Architects
2849 California St.
San Francisco, CA 94115
www.butlerarmsden.com

Cape Associates
345 Massasoit Rd.
Eastham, MA 02642
www.capeassociates.com

Chester Architecture LLC
8080 NE Beck Rd.
Bainbridge Island, WA 98110
www.chesterarchitecture.com

DRAW Architecture + Urban Design
405 Southwest Blvd, Suite 200
Kansas City, MO 64108
www.drawarch.com

DSDG, Inc.
1348 Fruitville Rd.
Sarasota, FL 34236
www.dsdginc.com

Glen Irani Architects Inc.
410 Sherman Canal
Venice, CA 90291
www.glenirani.com

Greener Lives LLC
P.O. Box 16157
Tucson, AZ 85732
www.greenerlives.net

Green Lyfe
1550 Willmar Ave. SE
Willmar, MN 56201

Hubbell & Hubbell Architects
1970 Sixth Ave.
San Diego, CA 92101
www.hubbellandhubbell.com

Kevin Oreck Architect, Inc.
113½ N. La Brea Ave. Suite 114
Los Angeles, CA 90036
www.kevinoreckarchitect.com

KieranTimberlake
841 North American St.
Philadelphia, PA 19123
www.kierantimberlake.com

Kipnis Architecture + Planning
1642 Payne St.
Evanston, IL 60201
www.kipnisarch.com

Krupnick Studio
10 A Valencia Rd.
Sante Fe, NM 87505
www.krupnickstudio.com

Levitt + Moss Architects
Santa Monica, CA 90405
www.levittmoss.com

LineSync Architecture
14 Castle Hill Rd.
Wilmington, VT 05363
www.linesync.com

LivingHomes
2910 Lincoln Blvd.
Santa Monica, CA 90405
www.livinghomes.net

MyGreenBuildings, LLC
205 N. Orange Ave. Ste. 1 SE
Sarasota, FL 34236
www.mygreenbuildings.com

Nathan Good Architects PC
205 NE Liberty St.
Salem, OR 97301
www.nathangoodarchitects.com

Pill-Maharam Architects
Shelburne, VT 05445
www.pillmaharam.com

Praxis Design/Build
1012 Marquez Place, Unit 310B
Santa Fe, NM 87505
www.praxis/designbuild.com

Richard Renner | Architects
35 Pleasant St.
Portland, ME 04101

133 South Main St.
Sherborn, MA 01770
www.rrennerarchitects.com

Robert Nebolon Architects
801 Camelia St., Suite E
Berkeley, CA 94710
&
143 First Court, Suite 1
Hermosa Beach, CA 90254
www.RNarchitect.com

Sarah Barnard Design
1507 7th Street # 093
Santa Monica, CA 90401
www.sarahbarnard.com

Srusti Architects
18524 Montpere Way
Saratoga, CA 95070
www.srustiarchitects.com

Studio 804
Marvin Hall
1465 Jayhawk Blvd., Room 105
Lawrence, KS 66045
www.studio804.com

Virge Temme Architecture
9098 Lime Kiln Rd.
Sturgeon Bay, WI 54235
www.virgetemme.com

Wolf Architects
98 North Washington Street
Boston, MA 02114
www.wolfarchitects.com

ZeroEnergy Design
156 Milk St., Suite 3
Boston, MA 02109
www.zeroenergy.com

Index